Landmark Visitors Guide

Dordogne

Mike Smith

The Author

Mike Smith spent seven years as headteacher of one of the country's leading comprehensive schools and three years as the proprietor of an antiquarian bookshop, before he became a magazine journalist and travel writer. He is the features editor of the lifestyle magazine Living Edge and the author of several topographical books and guidebooks, including France from the Channel Ports and Spirit of the High Peak, both published by Landmark.

Mike lives in the Peak District with his wife and daughter, but spends part of every year in France. He is a frequent visitor to the Dordogne.

How to use this guide: see page 5

Dordogne

N W E S

NONTRON
①
St-Jean-de-Côle
THIVIERS
Jumilhac-le-Grand
D708
D675
D704
BRANTÔME
Bourdeilles
RIBÉRAC
Sorges
N21
Excideuil
D705
L'Auvézère
Hautefort
La Dronne
D939
D730
PÉRIGUEUX
Échourgnac ③ D709
D708
N89 ②
MONTIGNAC
N89
L'Isle
Mussidan
N21
Rouffignac
Vézère
⑦
D710
Salignac-Eyvignes
LE BUGUE
Les Eyzies
D704
N20 Martel
D709
⑤
SOUILLAC
N140
D708
D703
St-Cyprien
SARLAT
D703
⑧ Carennac
BERGERAC
Trémolat
D703
Beynac
Rocamadour
D936
Dordogne
Dordogne
④
Cadouin
La Roque-Gageac
D933
N21
Monbazillac
D660
D710
Domme
⑥
Monpazier

0   20 miles

0   20 km

KEY

THE FOUR PÉRIGORDS

☐	Green Périgord	(see p 23)
☐	White Périgord	(see p 58)
☐	Purple Périgord	(see p 74)
☐	Black Périgord	(see p 106)

① Châteaux Country Tours   (see map on p 30)
② Périgueux Town Trail   (see map on p 50)
③ Touch of Venice Tour   (see map on p 63)
④ Bastides Tour   (see map on p 78)
⑤ Sarlat Town Trail   (see map on p 98)
⑥ Heart of the Dordogne Tour   (see map on p 110)
⑦ Cradle of Mankind Tour   (see map on p 119)
⑧ Pilgrimage Tour   (see map on p 131)

Contents

How to use this guide

The Dordogne region is one of France's most popular holiday destinations. French tourist publications usually use the pre-Revolution name of Périgord to describe the area.

This guidebook covers the four recognised tourist regions of Périgord. All the main attractions, and some lesser known ones, are described.

Each tour contains an easy-to-follow, loosely-themed round trip centred on a base chosen for its geographical location, available accommodation and possibilities for shopping and recreation. A Top Tips section is provided at the beginning of each tour, which lists attractions which are not to be missed, and things to do.

Four chapters cover the Green, White, Purple and Black Périgord regions, and walking trails around the fascinating old towns of Périgueux and Sarlat are also included.

First-time visitors may wish to concentrate on the Black Périgord areas, described in the Sarlat Town Trail and in the Heart of the Dordogne and Cradle of Mankind tours, but all the regions are worthy of lengthy visits.

The FactFile contains essential information for tourists. Opening times and telephone numbers of attractions and activity centres, hotels and campsites in the area, a selection of restaurants and details of markets and supermarkets can be found in the Additional Information at the end of each chapter.

Welcome to
The Dordogne

Some holiday regions are known for their spectacular scenery and the opportunities they provide for outdoor activities. Other tourist destinations are visited for their picturesque towns and villages, or their country houses, or their ancient castles. But there is one holiday area in south-west France that has everything. The Dordogne, also known by its pre-Revolution name of Périgord, possesses all manner of natural and man-made attractions in abundance.

English people can gain some idea of the region's intoxicating charms by imagining a heady cocktail of Peak District scenery and Cotswold architecture. The landscapes of the Dordogne are characterised by beautiful rivers, limestone cliffs, natural caves and ancient shelters, and much of the exquisite vernacular architecture of the region is fashioned in the sumptuous golden stone of the district. But there is much more: large tracts of Périgord are covered by extensive woodlands which contain a rich variety of wildlife; the celebrated regional cuisine includes some of France's most delicious dishes and there is easy access to some of the country's finest vineyards.

Tourists are often misled by travel brochures and information leaflets

Colourful Dordogne (The four Périgords)

The French Tourist Board markets the Dordogne as four regions: *Périgord Vert* (Green Périgord) in the north, with its woods, streams and splendid châteaux; *Périgord Blanc* (White Périgord) in the centre, with its limestone plateaux, wide valleys, forests and lakes, and its surprising touches of Venice in the towns of Périgueux and Brantôme; *Périgord Pourpre* (Purple Périgord) in the south-west, with its amazing conglomeration of *bastides* and its wine region around Bergerac; and *Périgord Noir* (Black Périgord) with its clinging villages, medieval castles, beautiful river scenery, and the remarkable survivals from prehistory that have given it a reputation as the Cradle of Mankind.

Black Périgord is the most visited area and is synonymous with the Dordogne for many people, but the other three regions offer equally wonderful sights and less traffic.

which make exaggerated claims for the qualities of quite ordinary places. Writers of travel guides have a duty to supply good, honest information, to avoid the unnecessary use of superlatives and to tell it like it is. In compiling this guide, I have not shirked from that responsibility but, having travelled the length and breadth of France over a number of years, I have no hesitation in testifying that the Dordogne is a very special place. Let us examine the evidence.

Caves

The Dordogne has the most remarkable collection of prehistoric caves (almost fifty) in France. Many contain colourful cave paintings which, together with artefacts gathered in or near cave shelters, form some of the oldest tangible evidence of man's developing intelligence. The unearthing of skeletons of Cro-Magnon man and the discovery nearby of primitive shelters and graves, has made Les Eyzies one of the most important centres for the study of prehistory in the world.

TOWNS AND VILLAGES

Man's imprint above ground in Périgord is no less remarkable. As the region's rivers have cut deep gorges in the landscape, there is little room for settlement along the valley floor, so riverside villages have to cling to the sides of almost vertical cliffs.

These gravity-defying settlements equal the perched villages of Provence with regard to spectacular location and daring construction, but surpass them in terms of architectural quality and the beauty of their natural materials. Clinging villages, such as Limeuil, Beynac and La Roque-Gageac, are superb illustrations of the slow evolution, over the centuries, of primitive cliff-side cave dwellings into beautiful houses, fashioned from the very rocks on which they stand. Forget Le Corbusier's description of the house as 'a machine fit to live in': these village homes are 'art forms fit to live in'.

The pilgrimage town of Rocamadour, more daringly attached to its cliff than any other village, has been one of the most visited places in France for 900 years. Some settlements in much quieter and less spectacular locations also rank amongst the most beautiful villages in the country. Carennac, in the Black Périgord, and St-Jean-de-Côle, in the Green Périgord, are my own favourites. The Dordogne is also known for its *bastides*, medieval towns built to a geometric plan around a large central square. Domme is the most picturesque of the *bastides* and Monpazier the most perfectly preserved.

Sarlat is the finest Renaissance town in France. It also possesses a large number of restaurants and one of the greatest open-air markets in a country noted for its markets. The Old Town area of Périgueux is not too far behind in the quality of its Renaissance survivals and the city also possesses a litter of Roman remains.

Brantôme, a beautiful island town north of Périgueux, brings a touch of Venice to south-west France.

CHURCHES

The Dordogne region contains some of the most bizarre ecclesiastical buildings in France. There are no less than 800 village churches in the region and many have a bulk disproportionate to the size of the community they serve. Those churches which have survived from the Romanesque (Norman) period, and there are lots of them, have very imposing exteriors with decorated, round-arched windows and doors, although their interiors can be disappointingly plain and dull. There is nothing dull about the cathedral of St-Front at Périgueux: it is the strangest cathedral in the whole of France. Some love it, some hate it, but no one can ignore it!

Châteaux

It will come as a surprise to many people to learn that Périgord has a larger number of châteaux than the Loire Valley – over 1,000 in total. They range from towering medieval fortresses to beautiful Renaissance houses, many of which retain defensive elements as decorative features. This plethora of fortifications is a legacy of centuries of Anglo-French rivalry and testimony to man's territorial obsessions and seemingly incurable belligerence.

A TURBULENT PAST

From Celts to Romans

From the sixth century BC until the Roman occupation, the Périgord region was inhabited by four Celtic tribes. The modern name of Périgord is a corruption of *Petrocorii*, the Celtic clan which had their headquarters at Vesunna, on the site of the modern city of Périgueux.

The Roman infiltration of south-west France was already evident by the second century BC, but Caesar began the invasion of Périgord in earnest in 59 BC. Eight years later, the last pockets of resistance had been eliminated.

In 16 AD, Emperor Augustus created the province of *Aquitania* (land of the waters) and developed Vesunna, which became known as Vesunna Augustus, as one of his regional capitals. Carduca (now known as Cahors), in the Lot region, was another major centre.

The Romans laid the foundations of a new agricultural economy in Périgord, by introducing walnuts, chestnuts, cherry trees and, of course, the vine.

By the third century, Franks and Alamans from the north were raiding Roman Gaul in some numbers. The Romans built walls around Périgueux and staged a last-ditch defence against the Barbarian hordes, but the Roman Empire was in terminal decline and by 420 the Visigoths had established control.

Périgueux has a good number of Roman remains, but there are surprisingly few survivals elsewhere in the

Continued on page 13...

France: Dordogne

Above left: Sizing up the menu
Above right: Cycling in the Dordogne

Left: Idyllic hotel at Brantôme
Below: Messing about on the river

Opposite page: The River Dordogne from the belvedere at Domme

The fun starts here

Tourists who travel to and from the Dordogne by car could be said to lose four days of their holiday in journey time. The secret, of course, is to make motorway travel fun and treat the journey as an enjoyable part of the holiday.

Caravanners require an overnight stop on their journey south, but many do not bother to leave the motorway in search of a caravan site. At *aires* and service stations no-one seeks to prevent tourists from dropping the steadies of their caravans and settling down for a free overnight stay. In fact, between dusk and dawn in the summer months, many service stations take on the appearance of a well-equipped caravan site! However, it should be emphasized that the Caravan Club advises members not to stay overnight in *aires* and service stations.

Travelling on the motorway itself can be quite entertaining and a fun part of the holiday. Different stretches of *autoroute* are administered by different companies and each company tries to put an individual stamp on its particular section. For example, the Calais-Amiens autoroute has an environmental theme, with the carriageway running between green embankments and under quaint, but newly-constructed, double-arched bridges clothed in vegetation. There is even a service station (near Abbeville) which is fuelled by wind power. In fact, this service station, with its lakeside walks, spectacular sunsets (if you are lucky!) and an observation platform with extensive views over Picardy, makes a good last stop on the journey home.

British motorways seem to be designed to offer the motorist minimum distraction and journeys on them can be very boring, but French *autoroutes* present drivers and passengers with many distractions. Valleys are crossed via spectacular viaducts, elevated sections give extensive landscape views, and there is any number of huge roadside sculptures. Brown tourist signs, which act like a guidebook for passengers as they pass through the French countryside, appear at frequent intervals. They do not simply label nearby attractions, but carry enormous realistic depictions of castles, churches and tourist sights. Although the drawings are informative and enticing, I am always somehow uneasy about them, feeling as if I am buying the postcard before I have made the visit.

Driving on French motorways is rarely dull. Make the most of the four days which you spend on them!

Dordogne region. However, south-west France is still known by its Roman name, slightly corrupted to *Aquitaine*, and present-day agricultural activity largely results from initiatives made by the Romans 2,000 years ago.

From Franks to Barons

In the years following the departure of the Romans, the region was torn apart by Frank and Visigoth rivalry. Clovis, King of the Franks, finally assumed control of Aquitaine in 507. A Saracen attack was repelled in the eighth century, but the Vikings made terrifying raids in the following century and soon occupied much of Périgord.

Christianity prospered under Charlemagne, who was crowned King of the West in 800, and several Benedictine monasteries were established in the region, although many suffered sacking and pillaging at the hands of raiders. However, a further period of ecclesiastical building, which lasted into the twelfth century, saw the establishment of abbeys, at places such as Chancelade, Cadouin and Rocamadour, and the construction of a vast number of Romanesque churches.

By the tenth century, Périgord was in the hands of powerful barons, whose persistent feuding and rivalries led to the building of strongholds at places such as Beynac, Biron and Bourdeilles.

The troubled marriage of France and England

Périgord's longest-running troubles began when Eleanor of Aquitaine married Henry Plantagenet, immediately after her divorce from Louis VII. Eleanor presented Aquitaine, which she had inherited from her father, as dowry to her new husband. When he became King of England in 1154, Henry pointed out that Aquitaine was now legitimately joined to the English throne. Needless to say, this statement did not go down too well with the French, but Henry and his son, Richard the Lionheart, continued to assert their claim to the region.

Richard was killed at the Siege of Chalus in 1199; King John was driven from France shortly afterwards and the French monarch then reasserted control over Aquitaine. The thirteenth century saw additional turmoil in Périgord with the Albigensian Crusade, waged by Simon de Montfort against the Christian sect at Albi.

The ding-dong battle for ownership of Aquitaine swung England's way in 1259, when the Plantagenet lands of Périgord and Quercy were returned to the English throne by Louis IX under the Treaty of Paris. A period of relative calm followed until Philip VI confiscated the English-held Duchy of Guyenne in 1337 and Edward III of England proclaimed himself King of France in 1340.

One hundred years of conflict

These conflicting claims initiated the Hundred Years' War, which actually lasted, on an intermittent basis, for 108 years!

The English had an early success at Crécy in 1346, but this did not prevent further conflict. The people of

Above: La Roque-Gageac

Below left: Cycling is very big in the Dordogne
Below right: Helpful gendarme, Souillac

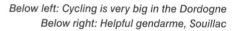

Bordeaux, with an eye on the profitable wine trade with England, asked Edward III for help. Edward responded by sending his son, Edward of Woodstock, known as the Black Prince, to crush the French armies. The Black Prince won a resounding victory at the Battle of Poitiers in 1356 and even succeeded in capturing King Jean II.

Under the Treaty of Brétigny, in 1360, the French obtained Jean II's release by ceding Aquitaine to the English. The region remained in English hands for nine years until Bertrand du Guesclin, Constable of France, recovered Périgord for the French. Battle was now well and truly joined once more. Various local warlords came down on one side or the other, but they were not averse to swapping sides when it was in their interest to do so.

Henry V, who had married the French king's daughter, Cathérine de Valois, won a decisive victory at Agincourt in 1415. Under the subsequent Treaty of Troyes, France was divided up between Henry, Philip the Good and the Dauphin. Partition almost always leads to further conflict, and this was no exception. When Henry died, the Dauphin declared himself King, Joan of Arc rallied the French forces, and the English were finally defeated and driven from France at the Battle of Castillon, near Bordeaux, in 1453. The Hundred Years' War was over at last!

Protestants versus Catholics

A century after the end of the Hundred Years' War, another protracted conflict began. This time, religious differences, brought about by the Reformation, were at the heart of the problem.

Cooling off in the pool at St-Avit-Loisirs, Le Bugue

Marriages of convenience

Eleanor of Aquitaine was a beautiful, passionate, independent and energetic woman, who wielded a huge influence over the course of events in Périgord.

In 1137, at the age of 15, Eleanor married Louis VII. The new Queen's dowry included the province of Aquitaine, which she had inherited from her father, William X. Eleanor had two daughters by Louis and she even accompanied him on the Second Crusade, but she grew tired of the King, complaining that she had 'married a monk'. Louis also grew jealous of Eleanor, who wished to live life to the full, and their marriage was annulled in 1152. The Queen cleverly managed to hold on to her dowry in return for Louis keeping the children.

Unbeknown to Louis, 30 year-old Eleanor had fallen for 18 year-old Henry, the son of Geoffrey Plantagenet. Eleanor married Henry just eight weeks after her divorce, and passed her dowry to him. When Henry became King of England in 1154, Aquitaine naturally passed into the hands of the English crown.

Eleanor, who loved art and politics, court life and life in general, inspired the troubadours and their ballads. The King and Queen had eight children, including Richard the Lionheart, Joan, who married the King of Sicily, and Eleanor, who married the King of Castille. Henry, meanwhile, was having affairs with a number of women, some of whom bore him children. Eleanor, in return, encouraged her sons to rise up in battle against her husband's rule, and Henry then responded by keeping his wife virtually locked up in a tower.

After Henry's death, Eleanor became adviser to Richard, her favourite son, whom she had set up as governor of Aquitaine, and she even took over administration of his kingdom during his long absences. At the age of 80, and still scheming, she travelled over the Pyrénées to bring her granddaughter, Blanche of Castille, to marry the son of the French king, with the aim of making peace between the Plantagenets and the Capetians. Another marriage of convenience!

There was a massacre of Protestants at Cahors in 1562 and 20,000 Huguenots, who had travelled to Paris for the wedding of Henry of Navarre on St Bartholomew's Day, 1572, were also massacred. The Wars of Religion then ensued. Atrocities were common, especially in south-west France, where villages and towns rallied to one side or the other. Bergerac was staunchly Protestant, but Périgueux was a Catholic stronghold.

Henry of Navarre, who was crowned Henry IV in 1594, converted to Catholicism, but gave the Huguenots freedom of worship under the Edict of Nantes in 1598. However, the treaty was revoked in 1685 and the Huguenots had to flee the country. Meanwhile, the peasants, known as *croquants*, after the *cros*, a bent pitchfork which they used as a weapon, were in revolt against crippling taxes and unscrupulous landlords.

Death of the Vines

The eighteenth century saw a period of prosperity. Town planning projects were carried out, the iron industry flourished around Nontron, the paper-making industry developed, and crop rotation was introduced. A plan to make Bergerac, Sarlat and Périgueux rotating capitals of the new *départment* of the Dordogne, created in 1790, was quickly abandoned and Périgueux became the one-and-only capital.

All seemed to be going well until disaster struck in 1868, when phylloxera, a pest which attacks the roots of the vine, ruined the wine industry. A mass exodus of peasants followed.

Exodus and influx

Depopulation continued to be a problem in the twentieth century and this was not helped by the death of 40,000 men from the Dordogne region in World War I. After the fall of France in World War II, the Dordogne was administered from Vichy France, but became a centre of the Resistance. The Germans retaliated by carrying out massacres at a number of villages, including Mussidan.

The introduction of large-scale tobacco growing somewhat revived the agricultural fortunes of the region, but depopulation was so bad by the Twenties that 10,000 Breton farmers were encouraged to move to Périgord and settle there. In recent years, a number of British farmers have also been drawn to the region.

The Dordogne today

The real saviour of the Dordogne has been its development as a tourist region, greatly helped by the discovery of the Cro-Magnon skeletons in 1868 and the unearthing of the Lascaux cave paintings in 1940. The ever-growing annual influx of tourists is bringing prosperity back to the area. Visitors arrive in their millions to enjoy the natural beauty and the superb buildings of Périgord, including the finest castles and fortified towns in France which, ironically, are a direct legacy of all those centuries of terrible conflict!

Scenery and recreation

There are no large cities to spread their urban sprawl across the countryside and the Périgord landscape is the most varied in France: a rich mosaic of wide valleys and deep gorges, thick woods and bare cliffs, white limestone and golden rocks, fast-flowing streams and tranquil lakes. The region is a playground for the pursuit of every type of outdoor activity imaginable. General information about outdoor activities appears in the FactFile at the end of the book and more detailed information is given in all subsequent chapters.

From ape-man to artist

In the early years of the nineteenth century, the French pioneered the study of prehistory. The Dordogne region was their favoured spot for research, and with good reason; the caves of the Vézère valley alone yielded over 100 prehistoric deposits which helped unravel the story of early man.

The earliest hominoid skeletons found on the African continent are some 3 million years old. As ape-man gradually evolved into *homo erectus*, posture became more upright, brain size increased, and manipulative skills, tool-making ability and communicative faculties all developed.

It is thought that 'upright man' crossed into Europe about 1 million years ago, via land bridges which then connected Africa and Italy. As the temperature of the planet cooled, about 600,000 years ago, *homo erectus* adapted by taking shelter in caves, by using animal skins for clothing, and by making controlled fires for warmth and cooking.

Almost every cave in the Dordogne region shows evidence of prehistoric habitation, and some of the remains date from 100,000 years ago when Neanderthal man, small of stature and with a receding forehead and emphasized jawbone, was the dominant advanced primate species in Europe. A Neanderthaloid skeleton found at Regourdou, near Montignac, is some 70,000 years old.

Neanderthal man disappeared about 35,000 years ago, by which time *homo sapiens*, with the upright stance and skull structure of modern man, had arrived on the scene. Three skeletons found in the Cro-Magnon cave shelter at Les Eyzies in 1868 are some of the earliest examples of *homo sapiens* discovered in Europe. As *homo*

Not surprisingly, the Dordogne is crowded in high summer and it is also quite hard to escape from other English-speaking visitors and expatriates. But do not despair: there are many opportunities to get away from the honey pots and there are countless surprises waiting to be discovered off the beaten track.

WHERE IS THE DORDOGNE?

The Dordogne is a department of Aquitaine in south-west France, and is named after one of the rivers that flows through it. It is a large inland region, covering an area of 3,500sq miles (9,060sq km) between the Loire Valley, to the north, and the Pyrénées, to the south. Bordeaux and the flat coastal regions of the Gironde and the Landes lie to the west, and the Massif Central to the east. The lack of coastline is more than compensated for by the glorious rivers that cross the region, including the Vézère, Dronne, Isle and the Dordogne itself.

The French are fond of commemorating geographical landmarks, so it is worth noting that latitude 45 runs through the region, indicating that the Dordogne is

sapiens developed, tools and weapons became more sophisticated and man also discovered his ability for artistic expression, through the manufacture of jewellery, ornaments and cave paintings.

The earliest paintings found in the shelters of Périgord date from about 35,000 years ago, and the pictures at Lascaux, which are surprisingly sophisticated, both in their realism and their depiction of movement, date from about 17,000 years ago. The cave paintings of south-west France rank among the most remarkable finds in the world. As someone with a strong interest in art, I find that they more than compensate for a disappointing lack of major art galleries in Périgord, because they raise such fascinating questions about the origins of art. I am intrigued by the fact that almost all the pictures depict animals; portraits of humans are almost entirely absent. What motivated the primitive artists? Why did they choose to depict the animals outside their shelters rather than the humans inside them? Were their paintings a means of overcoming fear of the wild beasts which inhabited their world? Were the pictures made by men or by women?

exactly half way between the North Pole and the Equator.

Sarlat, the chief tourist town, is some 530 miles (880km) by road from Calais.

WHEN TO GO

The season, as they say, lasts from April to October. Some tourist attractions are closed outside these months.

Visitors are virtually assured of hot and sunny weather in July and August, with temperatures consistently in the high seventies fahrenheit (mid-twenties centigrade) and occasionally much higher. This is an ideal summer holiday climate: not so unbearably hot as on the Côte d'Azur to the south, but almost always shorts and T-shirt weather and warm enough for sitting out late into the evening. The fact that the Dordogne is a green and pleasant land indicates that there must be a fair amount of rainfall, but in the summer months most of this falls in a short, heavy bursts, usually in late afternoon. These storms often have the effect of clearing the air and allowing a muggy afternoon to give way to a pleasant, fresher evening.

There is a good chance of pleasant weather in May and June, when the Dordogne is less crowded. The woodlands, flowering heather and local produce are all at their best in Autumn.

Tourists should always remember to take warm clothing for cave visits.

SHOPPING

Shopping in the Dordogne is a pleasurable experience, even for people like myself who usually find it an irksome business. French shopkeepers take great care with the presentation of their goods and produce highly imaginative window displays. Shops are usually open from 8am to 12.30pm and from 2 to 7pm, or later in popular tourist spots. French bread and cakes are delicious; clothes and jewellery are very stylish; and Dordogne souvenirs include baskets, pottery, paintings, fossils, especially supposedly genuine ammonites, whose wide availability is almost too good to be true, *foie gras*, truffles, wine and bottles of fruit.

Sarlat has one of the biggest open-air markets that you will ever see, but local markets, even in the smallest of places, often fill every street in the village. Parking can be a problem, but I would encourage tourists to visit them at every opportunity; French markets not only provide excellent opportunities to purchase good local produce and crafts, they are wonderful social occasions and are often accompanied by street entertainment. It is also possible, through the free samples on offer, to have ample wine and nibbles without spending a penny!

France has 1,000 hypermarkets and 7,000 supermarkets. The buildings which house them usually have the architectural qualities of an aircraft hanger and are dreadful blots on the landscape. However, their interiors are often very inviting, with air-conditioned environments which contain cafés, bars, newsagents and a comprehensive range of shops, in addition to a large superstore. They offer value-for-money, easy one-stop shopping, a cool refuge in very hot weather and a good place to spend time on a wet day!

EATING AND DRINKING

For many people, the best way to experience the true ambience of France is to enjoy a leisurely drink at a pavement café. As the proprietor will make absolutely no attempt to rush you, even if the place is full, there is ample opportunity to read the news-

---

Wine centres

Bergerac is the wine centre of Périgord; its Sauvignon grapes produce both red and white wines. The most famous vineyards are centred on the Château of Monbazillac, where a strong, sweet wine is produced.

Wine centres close to the Dordogne region include Bordeaux, which has an enormous concentration of vineyards specialising in red wine production, and Cahors, famous for Black Cahors, which is actually a deep red wine.

A gourmet's paradise

The famous regional dishes of the Dordogne are based on local products:

• The truffle, *la truffe*, is a black, aromatic fungus which is commonly added to omelettes, *pâté* and poultry dishes, and is used to flavour stuffings and sauces. For those who are prepared to pay exorbitant prices, it can even be eaten on its own.

• Walnuts are used to make delicious walnut cakes, added to salads as walnut oil dressing, and eaten with cheese.

• Strawberries, which are exported in quantity from Périgord, are found in fruit juice, creams, ices, tarts, and eaten on their own.

• Thick, exotic soups are a Périgord speciality, especially *tourain blanchi*, a white soup which contains garlic, goose fat and egg, and *sobronade*, which contains pork and vegetables.

• Strong local cheeses (very strong!) are made from goat's milk or sheep's milk.

• *Confits* is the traditional form of home-cooking. It is essentially pieces of goose, duck, turkey or pork, cooked in their own fat. The dish originated as a means of preserving parts of the goose in the days before refrigeration.

• *Foie gras*, made from the grossly swollen livers of duck or geese, is the most famous Périgord speciality and the most widely advertised. The production of *foie gras* involves force-feeding the birds with ground meal and large quantities of whole corn for the last two or three weeks of their lives. This process triples, or even quadruples, the weight of the liver. Those people who are prepared to stomach these methods insist on telling me that *foie gras* is delicious.

• *Foie gras entier* is sliced from whole liver and seasoned; *bloc de foie gras* is made from bits of liver emulsified with water; *parfait* is 75 per cent liver; *galantine* is 50 per cent liver; and *foie gras* is also found in the form of *pâté*, *mousse*, and *médaillon*.

paper or simply people-watch. Most restaurants provide outside seating, usually on the pavement, but occasionally, and somewhat perilously, on the carriageway itself! To spend the greater part of a warm evening at a pavement table in the presence of good company, a delicious meal and a bottle of local wine, is joy indeed.

Périgord cookery is among the very best, even in a country which is noted for its food. Local specialities include truffles, walnuts, strawberries, soups, cheeses, *confits* and *foie gras*.

The cheapest supermarket wines are very cheap indeed, but still perfectly acceptable. Even verygood wines can be purchased at surprisingly modest prices.

More information about the Bergerac vineyards can be found in the chapter on the Purple Périgord.

Celebration Time

Tourists visiting the Dordogne region in the summer months will pass through many towns and villages festooned with paper decorations. These colourful, carefully-made embellishments are not simply confined to buildings and bunting: trees and shrubs are made to burst unnaturally into bloom with paper flowers which are so realistic that they demand a second look.

In a Europe threatened by a plague of uniformity, it is good to see a region which is resistant to infection. Local customs, festivals and traditions are alive and well in Périgord, and there is even an attempt to prevent the death of local languages. Every year a town is chosen to stage the *félibrée* festival in July: a meeting of a society of writers which was founded in the nineteenth century, with the aim of preserving regional languages. The Queen of Félibrée accepts the keys of the town and gives a speech in local dialect. The women wear embroidered shawls and long skirts and the men wear felt hats and black waistcoats; and everyone partakes of a vast feast which begins with *chabrol*, a soup of wine and stock served in a commemorative bowl.

Most towns also hold an annual festival to honour their patron saint. Apart from the obligatory vast feast and paper decorations, there is likely to be music, dance and possibly fireworks and a funfair.

Weddings are also great occasions in Périgord. The wedding party walks in procession through the village, there is much hooting of horns, and the bride and groom ride off in a brightly-painted vintage car, often of doubtful mechanical efficiency.

Other festivals and festivities are legion. They include: a notable wine festival at Lalinde in early August; a Festival of Mime at Perigueux in August and September; *festival des jeux du théâtre* at Sarlat in July and August; jazz at Montignac and Souillac in July; and a demonstration of high wire artistry at Castillonnes in mid-August.

1. The Green Périgord

The Green Périgord (*Périgord Vert*) is the first Dordogne region which is encountered by tourists on their journey south.

Hautefort: Fortress and town

Top Tips

The Green Périgord

Not to be missed

- The scenic drive along the **D78 to Jumilhac-le-Grand**
- The **château at Jumilhac-le-Grand**, especially under floodlight
- A visit to the **Museum of Gold** at Jumilhac-le-Grand
- A slow stroll around **St-Jean-de-Côle**
- A guided tour around the **grotto at Villars**
- A visit to **Puyguilhem château**
- A visit to the **Doll and Toy Museum** at Nontron
- A tour of the village and the castle at **Hautefort**
- A visit to the **Truffle Museum** at Sorges

Things to do

- Shop at the Saturday market at Thiviers or one of the other markets
- Hire a cycle at Thiviers
- Go swimming at Thiviers
- Horse ride from Jumilhac-le-Grand or Hautefort or Tourtoirac
- Ramble along the GR436 near St-Jean-de- Côle
- Have a meal in the square at St-Jean-de- Côle
- Picnic in the woods by the Grottes de Villars
- Have a drink in the Place Alfred Agard at Nontron
- Go fishing near Nontron
- Attend pottery classes at St-Jean-de-Côle or Villars
- Play pavement ludo at Excideuil
- Follow the marked walk around Hautefort
- Go truffle hunting at Sorges

The 'Green' label is an invention of the French Tourist Board, which is anxious to draw visitors to this area from the better known White and Black Périgord regions, but it is a most appropriate name. Green Périgord is a green and pleasant land, with rolling fields, lush pastures, chestnut forests and a scattering of farmsteads, towns and villages, all in harmony with the surrounding countryside, because they are constructed from local materials. This is an agricultural region, with vines, crops of strawberries and tobacco, and groves of walnuts and fruit trees. Green Périgord is also the truffle capital of France.

There are fewer recognised tourist attractions in the Green Périgord than in the countryside around Sarlat and Périgueux, and hence far fewer visitors and much less congestion, but the Green Périgord does contain one of the finest and most varied collections of castles in France, from the forts of the Middle Ages to Renaissance châteaux.

Three of the castles are outstanding: Puyguilhem is a carbon copy of a Loire Valley château, but somehow more feminine and delicate; Hautefort is massive, bold and intimidating; and Jumilhac is romantic in both appearance and history. Green Périgord is also the land of the troubadours, who played a major role in adding to the legends and romance associated with the castles.

France is teeming with beautiful villages, many of which have been lovingly and carefully restored. The Dordogne region, especially at its heart, has a large number of villages which have officially been included in 'les plus beaux villages de France'. St-Jean-de-Côle, in the Green

Rural France

In the minds of many people, France is a largely rural country populated by peasants, and many tourists visit the country in search of this imagined idyll. The reality is not so simple: the French are highly sophisticated and cultured people who have embraced high-tech developments more readily than most countries: their transport and telecommunications networks are very advanced and their recent architecture is daring and innovative. However, France's population density is one third that of Britain, so there are large stretches of unspoilt countryside and there is a surprising number of unspoilt villages and hamlets which seem to be almost untouched by the modern world. Green Périgord is the epitome of rural France.

Périgord, is not the most spectacular of them but, in my view, it is one of the finest: a place where the tourist can leave the bustle of modern life and find beauty, peace and tranquillity.

Nontron is the capital of the Green Périgord and a pleasant town on an impressive site, but Thiviers has been chosen as the base for our tours of the Châteaux Country, not because of its intrinsic merits, but because routes to the best châteaux radiate from the town like the spokes of a wheel. Three tours, all centred on Thiviers, are described in this section.

THIVIERS

Thiviers is situated 23 miles (37km) north of Périgueux, at the intersection of the N21 with the D707 Nontron-Excideuil road. Although Thiviers is an unpretentious market town with no major tourist attractions, I have a soft spot for the place. I like the fact that its people are not on show for tourists, but simply go about their daily business; I am attracted to its nice little market place, its interesting church and its neat château; and I am charmed by its painted tourist information board, which not only details the town's history, but also carries little illustrated advertisements for local businesses, from restaurants to electrical shops to dry cleaners.

On the market place, which is known as Place du Maréchal Foch, there is a good *syndicat d'initiative* and a small **Musée du Foie Gras**. The weekly Saturday market has an abundant supply of *foie gras*, truffles and walnuts, and is also a good place to see local life and hear the unfathomable local dialect.

The tall church, which fronts onto the market place, has architectural elements from many periods. The earliest stonework is Romanesque, the vaulting is sixteenth century, the bell-tower is a nineteenth century addition, and the entrance porch has Renaissance detailing. The carvings on the Romanesque capitals are the church's most celebrated feature, but some of them, including a representation of a monster devouring a human, are extremely grotesque. I much prefer the impish faces on the two iron fountains which flank the main entrance to the church.

The town's castle, Château de Vaucocour, stands immediately behind the church. The fortress seems somehow out of place in the heart of the town and it does not receive a particularly good write-up in guide books, possibly because it has been much altered and restored, but it is a neat building with pepperpot towers.

There is limited hotel accommodation in Thiviers and its environs, but enough to suit all tastes and pockets, and there is also a 3-star campsite in the area. Jean-Paul Sartre is the town's most celebrated regular visitor. He spent rather unhappy childhood holidays here with his grandfather, who is said to have ignored his wife for 40 years because she had no dowry.

Visitors can enjoy a good meal at the Auberge Saint-Roch; cycles can be hired on the Rue Lamy; there are local swimming pools; and the Champion and Casino supermarket chains have stores on the edge of the town.

Below left: Imp at the entrance to Thiviers church

Below right: Tourist information at Thiviers

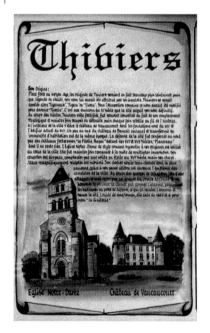

TOUR 1: CHÂTEAUX COUNTRY

Excursion to Jumilhac-le-Grand

'Outeaux' on a barn on the way to Jumilhac-le-Grand

We take the N21 from Thiviers towards Limoges. After 2.5 miles (4km), we fork right on the D78 for Jumilhac-le-Grand. The 9.5-mile (15 km) road to Jumilhac has lots of twists and turns, but is a very pretty road indeed, with lots of surprises along the way.

We soon come across a very long, extremely low building with a roof, almost at ground-level, which is punctuated by a line of *outeaux*, triangular openings designed for ventilation. A little way down the road, we see the very inviting Auberge de Combiers, and then pass through a tiny hamlet called **Montardy**, which has an incongruous, château-like house in warm brown stone. Beyond the settlement, there is an unexpected view of the River Isle, with a frothy weir and adjacent mill. We then travel through a dense wood and pass a roadside shrine before our sudden confrontation with the great **Château de Jumilhac-le-Grand**.

The château, which dramatically faces onto the vast village square, has a fantastic roofline of pepperpot towers, chimneys and turrets, topped by locally cast figurines of birds, angels and cupids, and depictions of the sun and moon. Gustave Doré, the celebrated nineteenth century artist and illustrator, called this the most romantic roofscape in the whole of France.

A fortress was first built on this site by the Knights Templars, but the core of the present structure was commissioned by Antoine Chapelle, a local ironmaster and armaments manufacturer, who was given the castle by a grateful Henry IV. A subsequent owner added two further wings.

The estate has a terraced garden and the castle itself has a fine seventeenth century master drawing-room, a stone staircase with Louis XV balusters and a Great Hall with a superb chimney piece, but the castle's main attraction is the Spinner's Room (*Chambre de la Fileuse*) where Louise de Hautefort was imprisoned by her husband.

The romantic castle is transformed into an illustration from a fairytale when it is floodlit. Late night visits can be made on Tuesdays and Thursdays during July and August and on Tuesdays during June and September.

In the village, there is an interesting little **Musée de L'Or** which tells the story of the local gold mines and gives information on the extraction and fashioning of the metal. There's gold in them there hills!

There are inns and gîtes in and around the village and there is a 2-star campsite in the vicinity. Markets are held in the huge square on the second and fourth Wednesday of each month; horse riding is available at the *Écuries de Jumilhac* and there are opportunities for fishing in the nearby river.

We can now retrace our steps to Thiviers, before taking our second tour.

The lonely spinner

A spiral staircase in the Château de Jumilhac leads to a room which is built into the wall of the castle.

The story goes that Louise de Hautefort was imprisoned in this room by her jealous husband who suspected her of infidelity. Louise is said to have passed the time spinning wool and weaving tapestries to decorate the room. According to legend, wool was brought to the prisoner by her lover, who had disguised himself in order to obtain work on the estate as a shepherd. This romantic story has an uncertain ending: some versions claim that the lover was captured and killed by Louise's husband; other versions have Louise reconciled with her husband, with the disappointed lover ending his life as a monk!

TOUR 2: CHÂTEAUX COUNTRY
Excursion to Nontron

Our second excursion from Thiviers takes us to Nontron, the capital of Green Périgord, via a pretty village, a colourful grotto, a delightful castle and an ancient abbey. We take the D707, signposted Nontron and Brantôme. Immediately after taking the right fork for Nontron (still the D707), we come across the boundary sign for **St-Jean-de-Côle**, but the turning to the centre of the village, which is to the right of the main road, is very easily missed. The narrow, cobbled street that gives access to the market place is immediately beyond Le St-Jean Hôtel. If you fail to spot this entry, make sure you turn back. St-Jean-de-Côle is too good to miss!

The village was once given an award for the 'best roofscape in France', beating off competition from all those Provencal hill villages with their rippled Roman-tiled roofs. This particular accolade surprises me, because it is quite difficult for visitors to actually see the roofscape: St-Jean-de-Côle is built on flat land, so it is only possible to obtain a good bird's-eye-view by climbing to the top of the church tower. But I can think of lots of other accolades which could have been given to this magical place.

The twelfth century church is very peculiar, but highly attractive. It is a nave-less, almost circular building, with a wooden ceiling, built to replace a collapsed dome, over its interior, and a covered market hall directly attached to its exterior. Wooden halls such as this are a common sight in the Dordogne, but it is rare for them to be built directly onto an ecclesiastical building.

Château de Martonie

The imposing **Château de Martonie** stands to the right of the church. The castle is a harmonious whole, despite its mixture of styles. The building was largely reconstructed in the sixteenth century, but two fourteenth century towers remain and there is a seventeenth century wing. Guided tours take visitors up a monumental

Church, market hall and castle all face onto a large open square, in which there is a simple war memorial. Across the market place, there are two inviting restaurants, Les Templiers and Restaurant le Coq Rouge, each with busy pavement tables, but the market square itself is strangely quiet and empty.

Just around the corner from the square, there is an unexpected and stunning street scene. Brightly-painted houses, all attractive, but in a variety of styles, flank a wide, straight road, whose concrete paving is studded with haphazardly-placed brown stones. The street tapers to a narrow, roughly-cobbled

Continued on page 32...

29

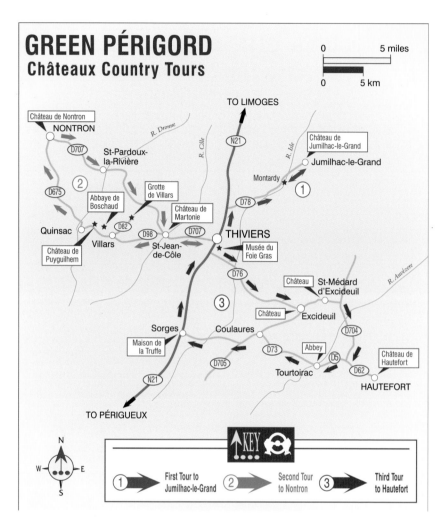

GREEN PÉRIGORD
Châteaux Country Tours

0   5 miles

0   5 km

TO LIMOGES

Château de Nontron
NONTRON

R. Dronne

R. Côle

N21

R. Isle

Château de Jumilhac-le-Grand

D707

St-Pardoux-la-Rivière

Jumilhac-le-Grand

Montardy

①

D675

②

Grotte de Villars

Abbaye de Boschaud

D78

Château de Martonie

Quinsac

D82

D98

D707

THIVIERS

Villars

St-Jean-de-Côle

Musée du Foie Gras

Château de Puyguilhem

D76

Château

St-Médard d'Excideuil

R. Auvézère

③

Château

Excideuil

Sorges

Coulaures

D704

Maison de la Truffe

D73

Abbey

D5

Château de Hautefort

D705

Tourtoirac

D62

N21

HAUTEFORT

TO PÉRIGUEUX

N
W   E
S

⬆ KEY 🔄
● ● ● ●

① First Tour to Jumilhac-le-Grand   ② Second Tour to Nontron   ③ Third Tour to Hautefort

*Old bridge,
St-Jean-de-Côle*

Les Plus Beaux Villages de France

Village street, St-Jean-de-Côle

The French attitude to building in the environment is strangely contradictory. The perimeters of many towns and cities are grossly disfigured by sprawling, badly-designed commercial centres and a plethora of huge advertising signs, and yet planners have gone to great pains to conserve and enhance hundreds of ancient villages and also Old Town areas in the larger settlements.

A typical village in lowland England has a variety of architectural styles and building materials, but most French villages are remarkably homogeneous in style and material. Bill Laws, author of *The Traditional Houses of Rural France*, claims that this has come about because 'rural people are both inherently conservative and frugally opportunistic'. For good economic reasons, almost all village buildings are constructed from local stone, and very often this is readily available. Once a local style evolved, builders tended to copy it over and over again, even adapting new materials and techniques to correspond to the particular style of the village. As a result, France possesses a huge collection of distinctive villages that blend into the landscape as easily as a rock outcrop.

The very best villages are given the accolade *Les Plus Beaux Villages de France* and are allowed to display a distinctive boundary sign.

lane which crosses the River Côle via a three-arched humpbacked bridge. The whole scene is unusual, colourful, and so very romantic and peaceful. St-Jean-de-Côle would make a perfect location for a honeymoon.

There is a little information centre and a small museum in the square and there are some nice, drunkenly-leaning half-timbered houses on the side streets. The GR436 gives access to good walks in the pleasant surrounding countryside.

One last recommendation: do not leave the village without visiting the public toilets! The spotless condition of these facilities is a clear indication that the people of St-Jean-de-Côle are very proud of their village and determined to take care of it. And rightly so!

After leaving the old village, we rejoin the main road and then take a left turn on the D98, which runs through nice wooded countryside to Villars. We can now take a 2-mile (3km) diversion by turning right along the D82 for the **Grottes de Villars**. Having reached a little hamlet, the road winds up through the woods to the cave entrance. (See box on Grottes de Villars below).

If we now retrace our route to Villars, we can take a side road to the **Château de Puyguilhem**. Like the entrance to St-Jean-de-Côle, this track is easily missed, so tourists should keep a careful watch for the signpost on the right-hand side of the road. The road climbs steadily for half-a-mile (1km) to a car park in the woods, leaving a 230yd (200m) walk to the château.

At a clearing in the woods we are confronted with a perfect image of a Loire Valley château. The appearance of the castle, built by Mondot de la Martonie in the early sixteenth century, is so surprising in this Périgord location, that the picture before us almost looks like a mirage. In true Loire Valley style, the building has mock fortifications and defensive elements, but is actually a very elegant country house.

The castle was restored in the Fifties and then refurnished with period pieces.

We now take the D3 in a north-westerly direction. A side road leads to the ruins of the **Abbaye de Boschaud**.

Grottes de Villars

The caves have a dazzling array of stalactites and stalagmites, some of which are bright yellow, and there are prehistoric wall paintings. The paintings, first discovered by the Speleological Club of Périgueux in 1953, were made 17,000 years ago and include, in the so-called 'Wizard and Bison' scene, a rare depiction of a human form. One painting of a horse has a neat blue outline, apparently due to calcite deposits.

There is ample parking here and there are lots of picnic tables in shady spots. There is a also a children's play area, a shop and a refreshment bar with patio seating.

Originally founded by Cistercian monks in 1154, the abbey fell into ruin after the monks were ejected at the time of the Revolution. The remaining buildings are substantial, but not particularly attractive.

After returning to the D3, we journey for about 1 mile (1.5km) before taking a left turn on the D98 for Quinsac. The dignified, white Château de Vaugoubert stands disdainfully above and beyond the settlement.

NONTRON

We shortly meet the D675 which passes through several hamlets of brown stone houses before climbing up to **Nontron**, which is superbly situated on a promontory between two ravines. From the little Place de la Résistance there are some splendid views of the Roman-tiled roofs of the Old Town.

A little further along the road, we arrive at a much larger square, the Place Alfred Agard, named in commemoration of a local benefactor. A great deal of effort has been put in to make the square a colourful and attractive place: neat paving is punctuated by bright blue bollards; there is a fountain with a small effigy of a cherub, a liberal provision of public seats and a pavement café. There is no parking in the centre of the square, but adequate roadside parking.

Château de Nontron

The eighteenth century **Château de Nontron** houses a doll and toy museum. The exhibits include a large dolls' house, many old parlour games and, somewhat incongruously, satirical marionettes of leading politicians created for the *Bebette Show*, a sort of French television version of *Spitting Image*.

Markets are held in the town on Wednesdays and Saturdays and there is a fair on the 18th of each month. Small pocket knives with boxwood handles are manufactured in the vicinity, and can be obtained from a number of shops. The town was formerly the centre of an iron and steel industry.

There are a number of hotels in Nontron, including the Grand Hôtel Pelisson, and there is a nearby 2-star campsite. The pleasant countryside around the town has good walks and also opportunities for fishing.

We can now return to Thiviers along the D707 which passes through St-Pardoux-la-Rivière and St-Jean-de-Côle. And who could resist stopping once again at the wonderful village of St-Jean-de-Côle before driving on to Thiviers?

Tour 3: Châteaux Country
Excursion to Hautefort

Our final excursion from Thiviers takes us to the most impressive castle of all: the massive fortress of Hautefort.

We take the N21 towards Périgueux, but then follow a left fork on the D76 for **Excideuil**, a little town with several points of interest.

Excidueil's church has a crown spire which immediately brings to my mind that of St Giles Cathedral in Edinburgh. The church was once a Benedictine monastery, but has been much altered over the years. There is a Romanesque statue of John the Baptist in the interior and an elaborate south doorway which dates from the fifteenth century.

The town's *syndicat d'initiative* and the 2-star Hôtel du Fin Chapon are both situated in a square at the foot of the château. Amusement is provided for children (and adults for that matter) of families who stop for refreshment at the

Excidueil's château

The château commands a limestone ridge which runs alongside the town. Périgord's troubled history is encapsulated in the story of this one building. Richard the Lionheart attacked the fortress on no less than three occasions in 1182. Having resisted these assaults, the castle then fell to the English in the Hundred Years' War, only to be recaptured by Bertrand du Guesclin. The Huguenots then took possession of the castle for a time during the Wars of Religion. In 1582, Henry III sold the building to François de Cars, who made the castle into a country residence by adding a Renaissance château.

The Black Pearl of Périgord

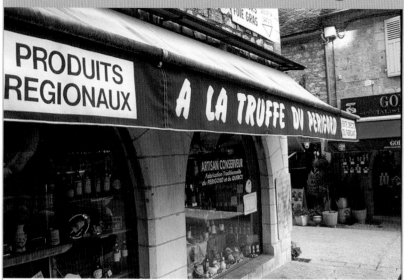

An objective description would suggest that truffles are black, lumpy blobs that grow underground on the roots of unhealthy trees, but gourmets have a very different view of this unpromising-looking fungus. The truffle has been the subject of much eulogising, with labels such as the 'Black Pearl of Périgord' and the 'Black Diamond of Cooking', implying that it is a jewel in the crown of French cooking. Claims have even been made for its aphrodisiac qualities.

Chefs use the truffle to garnish *foie gras*, omelettes and *pâté*. Because the fungus is regarded as a delicacy and is quite rare, it is expensive. The amounts used as garnish in a normal restaurant meal are likely to be fairly small!

The truffle grows mainly under oak trees, but also at the foot of lime and hazel. Experienced truffle hunters claim that they can spot where truffles are likely to be found by looking out for dead grass at the foot of a tree. Traditionally, specially-trained pigs were used to sniff out the fungus, but hunters nowadays often use dogs, supposedly weaned by bitches whose teats have been rubbed with truffle juice.

The power of poetry

The troubadours, who were very popular figures in the feudal courts, composed and performed lyric poems. Some of their compositions took courtly love, often unrequited, as their theme, but other songs were biting satires with political or religious content. Bertrand de Born, who was born at Hautefort in the twelfth century, was the most influential of the troubadours and often used his talent with mischievous intent.

Bertrand became Lord of Hautefort after ejecting his brother Constantine from the castle. When Constantine turned to Richard the Lionheart for help, Bertrand wrote lyrics designed to incite Henry Court-Mantel, Henry II's eldest son and heir to the English throne, into action against Richard. The chiding worked and Henry duly went to war, but with tragic consequences. Shortly after an attack on Rocamadour, Henry fell ill and died. With some justification, the King blamed Bertrand for his son's death and arranged for Richard and Alfonso II of Aragon to attack Hautefort. Bertrand surrendered, but put on such a convincing show of grief for Henry Court-Mantel's death when he was brought before the King that he was released.

After his release, Bertrand continued to compose and perform his lyric poems, many of which blatantly incited the barons to become warlords. He is said to have ended his days in a monastery!

hotel: a large ludo 'board' is marked out on the hotel's forecourt and giant chess pieces are provided as 'counters'.

Excideuil has a fountain donated by Marshal Bugeaud, the conqueror of Algeria; market day is Thursday, and there is a 1-star campsite in the vicinity. The D76 now joins the D705 which passes through **St-Médard-d'Excideuil**, where there is a domed Romanesque church and a **château** which was once the summer home of the writer André Maurois. When the D705 meets the D704, we head south along a good road until we see signs on our left for **Hautefort** via the D62. We turn left off the D62 to view the village and its great **château**.

HAUTEFORT

I recommend two circuits, one a perambulation, the other a short trip by car, to anyone who wishes to fully appreciate the remarkable assemblage of castle and village.

A marked walking route, which circumnavigates the vast perimeter walls of the castle, provides a study in contrast. The huge château glowers down on us from above, but we have extensive views over the pretty countryside below and the path takes us into the village of Hautefort, which is full of picturesque cottages, almost all of which are decked in colourful flowers. It is as if the inhabitants are determined to soften the scene and make the village an antidote to the grim castle.

I also recommend visitors to take a short car trip into the valley. Seen from the plain, the castle not only dominates the countryside for miles around, but seems to sit on top of its village like an elephant squashing insects under its weight. It is not so much the vast perimeter walls and the plain façades which give the château its intimidating appearance, but rather the great round towers with their Teutonic-looking domes. A copy of the domes even appears on the parish church, which was originally constructed as a hospital.

The bulk of the castle and the huge perimeter walls are enough to send a shiver down the spine, so it comes as a surprise, when we enter the castle, to find that it is really a fine sixteenth century residence, with tapestries, nice furniture, terraced gardens in the formal French style and a landscaped park in the less formal English style. There is a museum devoted to the novelist Eugène le Roy, whose father was bailiff here at the time of Eugène's birth in 1836, and a chapel containing the altar used for the coronation of Charles X at Reims.

A twelfth century fortress which stood on this site was home to the famous troubadour Bertrand de Born.

Market day in Hautefort falls on Wednesday. The Auberge du Parc offers 1-star accommodation and there is also a 1-star campsite in the vicinity. Horse riding is available at the *École Élémentaire d'Équitation*.

We now return to the D62 and retrace our route to the D704, where we take signs for **Tourtoirac**.

TOURTOIRAC & SORGES

The ruins of the eleventh century Benedictine **abbey** of Tourtoirac stand between the church and the river. I particularly like the flower boxes which have been placed in the Gothic niches at the entrance to the church.

Aurélie-Antoine, the self-proclaimed King of Araucania and Patagonia, died in the village in 1878. He left no heir but, over the years, various people have claimed succession to his 'throne'.

Horse riding is available at Les Tourterelles holiday centre.

We now take the D73 to Coulaures, where we travel a few miles south on the D705, before heading off on a right turn to **Sorges**, the Truffle Capital of Périgord. The **Maison de la Truffe** here provides a detailed initiation into the mysteries of the truffle and 'trufficulture'. If you arrive at the museum at 3.30pm on Tuesday or Thursday, you will be guided on a truffle hunt in the environs of the village. You are likely to visit Sorges outside the truffle season, but bottled truffles can be purchased here and some are preserved in Cognac. There are a couple of hotels in the town. Inevitably, one of them is called the Auberge de la Truffe!

After learning all there is to know about the black fungus of Périgord, we can return to Thiviers by the N21, and have truffles with our evening meal!

A corner of Hautefort

Additional Information

The Green Périgord

Accommodation

Hôtels

Excideuil
Hôtel du Fin Chapon *
☎ 05 5362 4238
11 rooms.

Le Rustic-Tourisme *
☎ 05 5362 4960
5 rooms.

Hautefort
L'Auberge du Parc *
☎ 05 5350 8898
5 rooms.

Jumilhac-le-Grand
Lou Boueiradour-Tourisme
☎ 05 5352 5047
4 rooms.

Nontron
Grand Hôtel Pelisson *
☎ 05 5356 1122
25 rooms, swimming pool, central
location.

St-Jean-de-Côle
Le Saint Jean *
☎ 05 5352 2320
5 rooms.

Sorges
Auberge de la Truffe **
☎ 05 5305 0205
18 rooms, swimming pool.

Hôtel de la Mairie *
☎ 05 5305 0211
8 rooms, swimming pool.

Thiviers
Hôtel de France et de Russe **
☎ 05 5355 1780
9 rooms.

Hôtel des Voyageurs-Tourisme
☎ 05 5355 0966
30 rooms.

Tourtoirac
Hôtel des Voyageurs *
☎ 05 5351 1229
12 rooms.

Villars
Les Relais de l'Archerie *
☎ 05 5354 8864
7 rooms.

Hautefort from the valley

Campsites

There are no 4-star campsites in
the Green Périgord or sites used by
organisations such as Eurocamp and
Keycamp, but the site at Tourtoirac has
chalets and mobile homes for hire, and
the municipal site at Thiviers is very well
equipped. The following campsites are
located on the Châteaux Tour routes.

Excideuil
Le Pont Rouge *
☎ 05 5362 4002
Municipal site, 33 emplacements.

Additional Information

Hautefort
Le Moulin des Loisirs *
☎ 05 5350 4655
50 emplacements, swimming pool

Jumilhac-le-Grand
La Chalonnière **
☎ 05 5352 573
33 emplacements, swimming pool.

Nontron
Le Stade **
☎ 05 5356 0204
Municipal site, 70 emplacements, swimming pool.

Thiviers
Le Repaire ***
☎ 05 535 26975
Municipal site, 100 emplacements, swimming pool, tennis.

Tourtoirac
Les Tourterelles **
☎ 05 5351 1117
93 emplacements, swimming pool, tennis.

Activity Centres

Jumilhac-le-Grand
Horse Riding
Les Écuries de Jumilhac
☎ 05 5352 5289

Attractions

Hautefort
Château
☎ 05 5350 5123
Open: 9am–12 noon, 2–7pm Palm Sunday to All Saints' Day; otherwise 2–6pm Sun and holidays; closed over the Christmas period.

Jumilhac-le-Grand
Château
☎ 05 535 24297
Open: 10am–7pm daily. Highly atmospheric night visits can be made 9–11.30pm on Tue and Thu in Jul and Aug and on Tue during June and Sept.

Musée de l'Or
☎ 05 5352 5543
Open: 10.30am–12.30pm, 2.30–6.30pm Jul and Aug. At other times of year open Sun and public holidays 4–6pm

Nontron
**Château de Nontron
(Doll Museum)**
☎ 05 5356 2080
Open: 10am–7pm Jul and Aug; 10am–12 noon, 2.30–6pm Jun and Sep apart from Tue; 2.30–6pm except Tue in Mar, Apr, May and Oct.

Puyguilhem
Château
☎ 05 556 2080
Open: 10am–7pm Jul, Aug, early Sep; 10am–12 noon, 2–6pm Apr, Jun, and early Sep to mid-Oct , closed Mon; 2–5pm Feb to Mar.

St-Jean-de-Côle
Château de Martonie
☎ 05 5362 3025
Open: 10am–12 noon, 2–7pm Jul and Aug.

Thiviers
Musée du Foie Gras
☎ 05 5355 1250
Open: 9am–6.15pm, apart from Sun Jul and Augt; closed daily for lunch and all day on Mon in May, Jun and Sep.

Villars

Grottes de Villars
☎ 05 5354 8236
Open: 10am–7pm in Jul, Aug; 10am–12 noon, 2–7pm Jun, Sep; 2–6.30pm Apr, May, Oct.

Eating Out

Nontron

Hotel Pélisson
☎ 05 5356 1122
Overlooking Nontron's bright and lively main square, has one of the best restaurants in town. Dishes are good value for money in terms of both quantity and quality.

St-Jean-de-Côle

Le Coq Rouge
☎ 05 5362 3271
Occupies a superb location on the edge of the old square in this highly picturesque village. The restaurant, which offers good local cuisine, is understandably popular, but prices are quite reasonable.

Sorges

Auberge de la Truffe
☎ 05 5305 0205
In the truffle capital of the Dordogne, is the obvious place to sample the Black Pearl of Périgord. Try the truffle omelette.

Thiviers

Auberge Saint-Roch
☎ 05 5355 0011
Has a nice homely atmosphere and serves up good regional dishes.

Tourtoirac

Hôtel des Voyageurs
☎ 05 5351 1229
Has a pleasant terrace restaurant overlooking the river. Local specialities are moderately priced.

Shopping

Market Days

Excideuil – Thursday
Hautefort – Wednesday
Jumilhac-le-Grand – second & fourth Wednesday of each month
Nontron – Wednesday and Saturday
Sorges – Friday
Thiviers – Saturday

Supermarkets

At the base town of Thiviers: Champion and Casino.

Syndicats d'Initiative

Excideuil	☎ 05 5362 9556
Jumilhac-le-Grand	☎ 05 5352 5543
St-Jean-de-Côle	☎ 05 5362 1415
Sorges	☎ 05 5305 9011
Thiviers	☎ 05 5355 1250
Villars	☎ 05 5358 6316

Tourist Information Centres

Hautefort	☎ 05 5350 4027
Nontron	☎ 05 5356 2550

Never judge a place on first appearances. My first encounter with Périgueux, a hurried drive through the town on a dull, drizzly day, left me with a vision of a huge, odd-looking church sailing on a sea of shabby, grey buildings. This negative image was so firmly planted in my mind that I made no attempt to make a proper examination of the place for many years. However, when I did finally make the effort, I was surprised and delighted to discover a town of narrow streets, old town houses, charming squares (both open and enclosed), a plethora of Gallo-Roman remains and a unique cathedral.

Top Tips

Périgueux

Not to be missed

- A visit to the **Cathedral of St-Front**
- A walking tour around the **Old Town of Puy St-Front**
- A walk around the **Cité** area in search of **Gallo-Roman remains**
- A visit to the **Musée du Périgord**
- **Son et Lumière** at the cathedral on Wednesday evenings (10.30pm)
- **International Festival of Mime** (early August)
- A stroll around the **night markets** on Wednesday evenings

Things to do

- Buy local produce in the fruit and vegetable market in the Place du Coderc
- Wine and dine in the Place St-Louis or the Galeries Daumesnil
- Take a guided walk from the Tourist Centre
- Contemplate the cathedral from a pavement café in the Place de la Clautre
- Take a 50-minute boat trip on the Isle
- Hire a canoe for a trip down the Isle
- Go ten-pin bowling or play billiards at Espace Wilson on the Rue Wilson
- Take a petit train ride from the Cours Montaigne
- Visit the cinema
- Visit the Military Museum
- Photograph or paint the scenes in the Old Town or the wonderful view from the river

Périgueux has a split personality in so many respects: the outskirts are rather messy and not particularly attractive, but the Old Town has some houses with architectural detailing every bit as fine as that on Sarlat's famous town centre mansions; the great Cathédrale de St-Front has the capacity to charm and infuriate in equal measure; Périgueux is a market town, but it is more industrial than any town in Périgord; and the settlement has two historically and geographically distinct centres that sit side-by-side on a hill above the River Isle.

HISTORY

Some years ago, I was ready to dismiss Périgueux as a rather unattractive semi-industrial town. Now, after getting to know the place much better, I am very happy to recommend it to you as worthy of a lengthy visit. Périgueux is not so self-consciously touristy as Sarlat and its Old Town is not so obviously prettified, but its architecture is very fine indeed, Roman remains are scattered about the *Cité* with almost careless abandon, and you will certainly want to visit that amazing cathedral and make up your own mind about the merits of the building!

Périgueux was founded by the *Petrocorii*, meaning four Celtic tribes, close to a sacred spring called the *Vésonne*, but it was the Roman occupation which brought a period of impressive development and prosperity. Temples, villas, baths, a forum, and a massive aqueduct were all constructed in the town, which became known as Vesunna. Unfortunately, many of these buildings were partially destroyed and ransacked for stone when the inhabitants built fortifications in an unsuccessful attempt to keep out the Barbarian hordes.

The citizens of Périgueux were converted to Christianity by St Front. The saint was buried on a hill (*puy*) immediately east of the old Gallo-Roman town and the church that was built on this site became a noted place of pilgrimage, especially after accounts of St Front's life became somewhat embellished and glamorised. Rivalry soon developed between Puy St-Front, the town that grew up around the church, and the original settlement on the site of the old Gallo-Roman *Cité* next door. The two towns were formally amalgamated in 1240 but this did not put an end to their separate identities or their rivalry. During the Hundred Years' War, Puy St-

Front was loyal to the French crown but the *Cité* sided with the English.

Périgueux was a Catholic stronghold during the Wars of Religion. Its cathedral was attacked and looted by the Protestants and the church of St-Étienne in the *Cité* area also suffered. However, the fifteenth and sixteenth centuries saw successful commercial development in the Puy St-Front area and the construction of the fine town houses that survive to this day. When the Dordogne was established as a department in 1790, Périgueux was nominated, together with Bergerac and Sarlat, as a prefecture on a rotating basis, but the town somehow managed to assume the role of regional capital on a permanent footing.

The coming of the railway in 1856 improved the prosperity of Périgueux, but also did some damage to its appearance. The railway put the town on a communication route and brought with it new industry in the form of a large repair yard, but the railway line cut a great gash through the old *Cité* area. Meanwhile, the architect Abadie was busy remodelling the Cathedral of St-Front in an ostentatious Byzantine style.

Modern Périgueux is a regional capital and market town. The railway repair yards are still there and France's postage stamps have been produced in the town since a decentralisation programme was enacted in France in the Seventies, but the most important development from a tourist point of view has been the restoration of the Old Town area around the cathedral.

WALKING TOUR OF THE PUY ST-FRONT QUARTER

There are various organised ways in which to see Périgueux. It is possible to board a tourist 'train' (*petit train*) in the Cours Montaigne for a leisurely trip around the streets of the old quarter. Those wishing to wander on foot can take in the best sights by following the network of brown tourist signs in the Puy St-Front and *Cité* areas, and there is a choice of three guided walks which leave the Tourist Office at different times of day. It is also possible to see Périgueux from the river by taking a cruise along the Isle. The walking trail described in this guide is a personally selected route around the most interesting streets in the Old Town.

See map on page 50

PLACE FRANCHEVILLE

Our tour begins at the Place Francheville where there is ample parking at a small charge. Although there is a two hour limit between 9.30am and 12 noon and between 2.30 and 4.30pm, parking is free between 12 noon and 2.30pm, so it is possible to leave the car from 10am to 2.30pm for a two-hour fee. Unless I have misunderstood the instructions!

The Place Francheville is cut in two by a large Monoprix store. From the pedestrian crossing on the east side of the store, it is possible to walk directly to the cathedral along the Rue Taillefer, a busy shopping street with a variety of attractive retail outlets. Those who are more interested in history and architecture than shopping can take an indirect route and meet up with the shoppers at the western entrance to the cathedral on the Place de la Clautre.

RUE DE LA BRIDE

Our tour for the architecture lovers begins at the Tourist Office at the southeastern corner of the Place Francheville where we take the Rue de la Bride which runs between the Tourist Office and the **Tour Mataguerre**, a bulky white tower with arrow slits and machiolations. The tower was once part of a defensive network of twenty-eight towers which protected the medieval city, and is said to take its name from an Englishman imprisoned here during the Hundred Years' War.

The first section of the Rue de la Bride, which evolves into the Rue des Farges, is rather dull and somewhat disfigured by graffiti; there is some

Above: Place St-Louis

Left: No 3 Rue du Calvaire

Opposite page: Flower shop, Rue de la Clarté

dilapidation and the Old Town atmosphere is hardly fostered by the incongruous presence of a sex shop and the Wales Pub. But do not despair: you are about to enter a fascinating maze of streets. The houses are very clearly numbered, there are helpful, wall-mounted explanatory plaques in French, German and English, and the Old Town is greatly enhanced by wall-hung street lamps and nice paving, cobbles and setts on the narrow carriageways. The French are so good at this sort of thing!

RUE DES FARGES

Numbers 4 and 6 on the Rue des Farges, collectively known as the **Maison des Dames de la Foi** (House of the women of faith), were founded in the thirteenth century but became a convent in the seventeenth century. Look upwards and you will see pointed arches topped by round arches, and round arches topped by a loggia. It is possible that Du Guesclin, who recovered Périgord from the English, stayed here during the Hundred Years' War. The Rue des Farges ends at the **Musée Militaire** which traces the story of Périgord's many conflicts through its considerable collection of weapons and uniforms.

RUE AUBERGERIE TO PLACE DE LA CLAUTRE

Turn right down the steep Rue Aubergerie where you will find a Greek restaurant, the Helleniko, and the Hôtel d'Abzac de Ladouze, a large turretted building with an impressive octagonal tower. A left turn now takes you along the Rue St-Roch. This short street has two little architectural treats: do not fail to cast your eyes up the plain façade of No 4, to catch an unexpected view

of an Italian-style arcaded loggio with diamond-shaped stone decorations, and make sure you glance down the Rue de Sully at the end of the Rue Aubergerie, to catch a glimpse of the peephole window above the door of the first house.

Turn left up the Rue de Calvaire, the 'Road to Calvary'. This is the street up which condemned men were taken on their way to execution in the Place de la Clautre. One wonders if the unfortunate prisoners appreciated the irony in the street name of the Rue Tranquille, which can be glimpsed on an alley to the right. Number 3 Rue de Calvaire has a superbly decorated Renaissance porch and a large studded wooden door.

At the head of the Rue de Calvaire you will emerge into the small Place de la Clautre where you can join the shoppers in your party who will have walked along the Rue Taillefer from the Place Francheville. It will be interesting to see who arrives first at the

St-Front Cathedral

There has been a church on the site of St Front's burial place since the sixth century. The original chapel was enlarged in 1047, only to be destroyed by fire in 1120. The replacement church, consecrated in 1173, was Byzantine in style, shaped like a Greek cross and domed. Its cupolas were similar to those of St Mark's in Venice. A further restoration was carried out after the Huguenots had inflicted damage on the church and its treasures during the Wars of Religion, but the building later fell into disrepair.

Yet another restoration, which virtually amounted to a rebuilding, was carried out to the designs of Paul Abadie between 1852 and 1901. Abadie tore down a great deal of the old church, but he retained the huge, tiered Romanesque bell-tower, and topped it with a pine-cone lantern, which he then cloned to decorate every single dome and pitched roof on the building. The cloning is somewhat overdone, but the repeated pinnacles do help to bring unity to the vast church, which is essentially a riot of domes and cupolas. Abadie certainly liked his pine-cone decorations, for he was soon using them again as lanterns for Sacré-Coeur in Paris.

You can enter the cathedral from the Place de la Clautre via a courtyard framed by gaunt walls which have survived from the old church. The rather plain and austere interior of the church is in marked contrast to the extravagant exterior, but there is some nice stained glass and there are some very ornate chandeliers designed in Byzantine style by Abadie himself. The west door is topped by a huge modern organ which was being played quite beautifully during my most recent visit. The interior is not as dark as Abadie's basilica of Sacré-Coeur in Paris, but the great carved walnut altarpiece, framed by pillars in the form of coiled snakes, remains in total darkness unless you pay a small fee for some illumination. The Baroque style of the altar, which is too heavy and overbearing for my taste, is repeated on the large carved pulpit.

Clones

By the mid-nineteenth century, the cathedral of St-Front had fallen into disrepair and a massive restoration project was needed to save the building. There was some suggestion that Viollet-le-Duc, famous as the restorer and embellisher of many damaged medieval survivals throughout France, might be employed at Périgueux, but the task was given to the architect Paul Abadie, who began work in 1852.

Abadie took the domed form of the old church as his inspiration, but cleared away old sculpture and decoration to create a feeling of immense interior space, whilst adding further domes and turrets, all topped by pine-cone cupolas. The plethora of domes is off-set by a single tall bell-tower, also topped by a pine-cone.

Abadie's work at Périgueux, which took half a century to complete, has been the subject of much criticism and ridicule. The building has been condemned for the supposed bareness and coldness of its interior; there have been complaints about the too-orderly cut of the cathedral's stone-work and those domes and pine-cones have attracted much scoffing. Freda White, author of *The Three Rivers of France,* described the church as grandiose and dead, and she called Abadie 'this deplorable builder who wrought havoc far and wide through south-western France in the mid-nineteenth century'.

Everyone is entitled to their own opinion, and I have to say that I rather warm to Abadie's bold and innovative design. The architect himself was so taken by his work at St-Front that he used all the same major architectural elements in his design for Sacré-Coeur in Paris, on which he began work in 1875. The Montmartre basilica has the same feeling of immense interior space as the cathedral of St-Front; it also has a single, tall bell-tower and a number of domes and turrets, all topped by those pine-cone cupolas. Critics have been rather kinder about the architectural merits of Sacré-Coeur, but if Abadie had not been inspired by the architectural forms he found in Périgueux, it is unlikely that Montmartre would now be crowned by such a distinctive landmark.

rendezvous point. Who will have been detained longer by the distractions along their route: the shoppers or the culture vultures?

Although the Place de la Clautre is a fairly small square, it is large enough to house a Wednesday and Saturday market and a winter truffle and *foie gras* market. The pavement cafés which flank the square make an ideal and timely refreshment stop and they provide an excellent viewing platform from which to contemplate the eccentric architecture of St-Front Cathedral. (see box on page 48).

Continued on page 52...

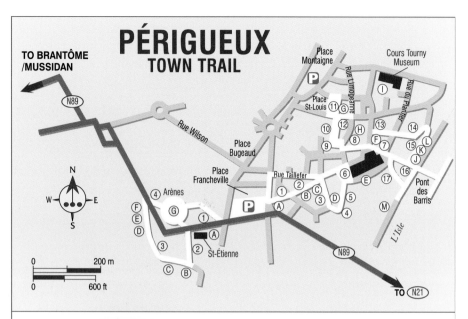

PÉRIGUEUX
TOWN TRAIL

Main route through Périgueux

Town Trails

CITÉ AREA

1 Rue de la Cité
2 Rue Romaine
3 Rue de Turenne
4 Rue de l'Amphithéâtre

Ⓐ Église St-Étienne
Ⓑ Tour de Vésonne
Ⓒ Villa de Pompeius
Ⓓ Château Barrière
Ⓔ Maison Romaine
Ⓕ Porte Normande
Ⓖ Arènes

PUY ST-FRONT QUARTER

1 Rue de la Bride
2 Rue des Farges
3 Rue Aubergerie
4 Rue St-Roch
5 Rue du Calvaire

6 Place de la Clautre
7 Rue Daumesnil
8 Rue de la Clarté
9 Place du Coderc
10 Rue de la Sagesse
11 Place St-Louis
12 Rue Éguillerie
13 Rue de la Constitution
14 Rue Barbecane
15 Rue du Port-de-Graule
16 Boulevard Georges Saumande
17 Rue Tourville

Ⓐ Tour Mataguerre
Ⓑ Maison des Dames de la Foi
Ⓒ Musée Militaire
Ⓓ Hôtel d'Abzac de Ladouze
Ⓔ Cathédrale St-Front
Ⓕ Maison de Daumesnil
Ⓖ Maison Tenant
Ⓗ Galeries Daumesnil
Ⓘ Musée du Périgord
Ⓙ Maison du Lur
Ⓚ Maison Cayla
Ⓛ Maison Lambert
Ⓜ Vieux Moulin

Above: Houses on the banks of the River Isle

Below: Fountain in Place St-Louis

RUE DAUMESNIL TO PLACE ST-LOUIS

If you leave St-Front Cathedral by the door in the north aisle you will emerge into the Rue Daumesnil where there is a rather grand eighteenth century house which is the birthplace of Pierre Daumesnil, who was one of Napoleon's generals in the Egyptian campaigns.

Turn left up the Rue de la Clarté where you will find some pavement cafés and a very attractive flower shop. The window and pavement displays at French florist shops are as daring in their use of colour and as full of *joie de vivre* as a Fauve painting. Turn right into the Place du Coderc and you will come across another colourful French scene: a fruit and vegetable market where you can buy local produce from local farmers or simply soak in the fascinating interaction between persistent sellers and perceptive buyers.

The Rue de la Sagesse leads to the Place St-Louis, a very different kind of Périgueux square. The *place* is crammed with the pavement restaurants and cafés where you can wine and dine under the shade of trees or large parasols. Further respite from the heat is provided by the clear, cool waters of a modern fountain, first placed here in 1980. But the archictural *pièce de résistance* of the Place St-Louis is the **Maison Tenant**, at the south-eastern corner of the square (see feature box below).

ON TO GALERIES DAUMESNIL

The Rue Éguillerie, which runs alongside the Maison Tenant, leads to the Rue Limogeanne. This street has two main attractions: very good opportunities for shopping, to both left and right of our point of entry, and some fine Renaissance architectural details on Nos 3, 5, 7 and 12. Look for an opening on the east side of the Rue Limogeanne and walk in to the **Galeries Daumesnil**, a little world of closed squares and linking alleyways completely shut off from the noise and bustle of modern Périgueux. This is an ideal place for an evening meal: inviting restaurants include La Calèche and Pizzeria Les Coupoles.

Maison Tenant

A cold analysis would suggest that this grand town house is a conglomeration of disparate bits and pieces: a tower with a pepperpot turret sandwiched between a mullioned and transomed windowed façade and a machiolated corner section. But the Maison Tenant possesses that brand of unaccountable harmony which often stems from the juxtaposition of contrasting styles. I love this building!

As you emerge from the Galeries Daumesnil you will come face to face with an antiquarian bookshop. The painted wooden front of the shop is as old as the books on sale inside and the unspoken invitation to browse is irresistible.

RUE DE LA CONSTITUTION TO RUE DU PORT-DE-GRAULE

Walk down the Rue de la Constitution, note the fanlight on No 3 and delight in the view of St-Front's domes down the Rue de Nation. Turn into the Rue du Plantier, which you could well find decked in "bunting" in the form of washing hung from the balconies of the old houses. A diversion up the Rue du Plantier would take you to Périgueux's **Musée du Périgord**, which houses an eclectic collection, including: Gallo-Roman remains from the old town of Vesunna; prehistoric finds from the area, including a 70,000 year old skeleton; manuscripts and documents from Oceania; and a collection of paintings and ceramics.

To continue the town trail, ignore the left turn to the museum and proceed down the Rue Barbecane. Steps on the right hand side of this street drop down to the Rue du Port-de-Graule, a claustrophobic street of old houses with very low doorways. It is common knowledge that the average height of human beings has increased over the centuries, but were people in medieval times actually small enough to enter these buildings without stooping?!

BY THE RIVER BANK

Walk up the steps at the end of the Rue du Port-de-Graule to the Avenue Daumesnil and then take a left turn to reach the Boulevard Georges Saumande and the quayside. Cross the bridge to the east bank of the Isle for a wonderful view of the great cathedral and a proper appreciation of three fine houses, **Maison Lambert**, **Maison Cayla** and **Maison du Lur**, which line the west bank of the river. The elaborate dormers, grand colonnades and carved balustrades of these mansions are an unashamed display of wealth and power.

Cross back to the west bank of the river and take a left turn to view the **Vieux Moulin**, an altogether improbable building, not simply because it is timber-framed in a city surrounded by plentiful supplies of stone, but because it sits on top of a narrow, tall podium of stone, like some bizarre exhibit in a sculpture park. However, there is a rational explanation for this surreal illustration of the physics of equilibrium: the stone podium is actually a surviving fragment of the old town wall onto which the mill, which was in the ownership of the cathedral, was built.

You can now complete the Puy St-Front town trail by walking up the beautifully-curved Rue Tourville to the cathedral and then taking the Rue Taillefer back to the Place Francheville.

The Belfry, St-Front

Roman relics

The old Gallo-Roman area of Périgueux is far less attractive than the
Puy St-Front district: a railway cutting
runs through the area; the **Église
St-Étienne-de-la-Cité** is one of the
ugliest churches you are ever likely to
see and some of the Cité's streets are
rather drab and shabby. However, the
cité is worthy of a visit, because it still
displays ample evidence of its days as
an important Roman town. Gallo-
Roman remains are scattered about
the area with almost careless abandon:
walk down almost any street, no matter
how uninviting, and you are likely to
come across a Corinthian column or
a fragment of a Gallo-Roman wall or

See map on page 50

the foundations of a Roman
town house.

Our tour begins at the Place
Francheville. Leave the car park
by walking down the Rue de
la Cité in a westerly direction.
The severe walls of St-Étienne
come into view on your left.
The church looks damaged
and badly truncated, and this
is hardly surprising when one
considers the attacks made
upon it by the Huguenots and
its loss of cathedral status in
the seventeenth century. The
interior is dark and dismal,
but it is worth adjusting to
the gloom, in order to study
the two domes, one elev-
enth century and one twelfth
century, and the seventeenth
century walnut altar.

Turn left down the Rue
Romaine to the **Tour de Vésonne**, a
60ft (17m) high cylindrical tower that
was part of a second century temple.
The great gash in the tower actually
provides a fine 'cutaway view' which
allows us to appreciate the excellence
of Roman building techniques.

Excavations carried out in the 1950s
immediately adjacent to the Tour de
Vésonne uncovered the foundations of
a Gallo-Roman house. The residence,
known as **Villa de Pompeius,** had a
heating system, baths and workrooms.

Turn right into the Rue de Turenne
to find the **Château Barrière**, a
castle with a twelfth century keep, the
Maison Romaine, essentially a scattering of Gallo-Roman architectural
survivals, and the **Porte Normande**,

No surrender!

Périgueux has a one-legged hero. Pierre Daumesnil, who was born in the city in 1776, fought with Napoleon at Arcola, in Egypt, and later lost a leg at Wagram, near Vienna.

After Daumesnil was rendered incapable of active service, Napoleon made him governor of the Château of Vincennes, in Paris. When Blucher demanded the surrender of the fortress in 1814, Daumesnil is said to have replied: "I'll surrender Vincennes when you give me back my leg." Another version has the governor shouting: "Tell them to give me back my leg or come and get the other one".

Whatever the correct version, Daumesnil flatly refused to surrender to the Allied attack, and he held firm again when a mob tried to storm the castle in 1830, in an attempt to lynch the ministers of Charles X who were imprisoned there. On this occasion, Daumesnil threatened to ignite the powder room if the mob tried to enter the château.

Daumesnil's statue, erected in 1873 in the Cours Montaigne, has the general proudly displaying his wooden leg. The Forest of Vincennes, now a Parisian public park, contains a lake known as Lac Daumesnil.

the remains of a city gate which is at least 1,000 years old and may have been built in an attempt to keep out the marauding Vikings.

Turn right along the Rue de l'Amphithéâtre to the public garden which occupies the site of a Roman arena (**Arènes**). The amphitheatre was the venue for gladitorial contests and had a capacity of at least 20,000. Drop down to St-Étienne and take the Rue de la Cité back to the Place Francheville.

Other activities in Périgueux

Canoes can be hired at Animation Isle Canoë Kayak for trips down the Isle river.

Périgueux is an excellent shopping centre and there are large out-of-town supermarkets. The city has ample hotel accommodation; there is also a youth hostel and a good campsite.

Périgueux is a lively city. There is an international contemporary mime festival in early August and regular concerts and recitals are held in the cathedral; Son et Lumière, illustrating the legend of St Front, take place at 10.30pm on Wednesdays in the summer; and there are themed night markets, with lots of musical accompaniment, on the Place St-Louis on Wednesday evenings. In the summer months, Périgueux seems to be constantly alive with the sound of music.

There is a regular programme of movies in town and there are billiard tables and a ten-pin bowling alley at Espace Wilson, 33 Rue Wilson.

Additional Information

Périgueux

Accommodation

Hôtels

Bristole Hôtel ★★★
☎ 05 5308 7590
29 rooms.

Hôtel Talleyrand Périgord ★★★
☎ 05 5354 3770
42 rooms.

Hôtel des Barris ★★
☎ 05 5353 0405
12 rooms.

Hôtel Ibis ★★
☎ 05 5353 6458
89 rooms, situated between the cathedral and the river.

Hôtel du Midi et Terminus ★★
☎ 05 5353 4106
23 rooms.

Hôtel du Périgord ★★
☎ 05 5353 3363
Member of the Logis de France chain, 20 rooms.

Hôtel Regina ★★
☎ 05 5308 4044
35 rooms.

Hôtel de l'Univers ★★
☎ 05 5353 3479
12 rooms.

Hôtel Wilson ★★
☎ 05 5309 3677
47 rooms.

Hôtel les Charentes ★
☎ 05 5353 3713
12 rooms.

Hôtel du Lion d'Or ★
☎ 05 5353 4903
10 rooms.

There is also a selection of hotels at the out-of-town commercial centre at Boulazac:

Hôtel Grill Campanile ★★
☎ 05 5309 0037
37 rooms.

B and B Hôtel ★
☎ 05 5306 6161
60 rooms.

Le Relax ★
☎ 05 5309 3128
Swimming pool.

Hôtel Formule 1 – Economique
☎ 05 5398 6200
63 rooms.

Campsites

Camping Le Grande Dague ★★★★
☎ 05 5304 2101
Chalets and mobile homes, swimming pool.

Youth Hostel

There is a youth hostel at Rue des Thermes, Prolongues, 24000 Périgueux 1. ☎ 05 5353 5205. 1.2 miles (2km) from the station and open all year.

Activity Centres

Boat Trips
Quai L'Isle
☎ 05 5324 5880
At foot of cathedral. On the hour between 10am and 6pm.

Canoeing

Animation Isle Canoë Kayak

☎ 05 5353 0672

Ten-pin Bowling

Espace Wilson

☎ 05 5303 9598

Attractions

Musée Militaire

☎ 05 5353 4736

Open: 10am–12 noon, 2–6pm Apr to Sep, closed Sun and holidays; 2–6pm Oct to Mar.

Musée du Périgord

☎ 05 5306 4070.

Open: 10am–12 noon, 2–6pm Jul, Aug, Sep closes Tue; closes at 5pm during the rest of the year

Eating Out

Anyone wishing to sample the famous Périgord cuisine is spoilt for choice in Périgueux. The city has a large number of restaurants offering local dishes. Given the choice available, it would be invidious to make particular recommendations. Visitors will wish to make their own explorations and discoveries. The following restaurants are mentioned simply to give a flavour of what is available:

Les Berges de L'Isle

☎ 05 5309 5150

Overlooks the river. The restaurant's specialities include *foie gras* dishes and a particularly wide range of desserts.

Hôtel Domino

☎ 05 5308 2580

On the Place Francheville, has a nice restaurant with good food at fairly reasonable prices.

La Flambée

☎ 05 5353 2606

On the Rue Montaigne, serves a particularly good range of regional dishes.

L'Oison

☎ 05 5309 9402

On the Rue St-Front, is a small restaurant with a big reputation. Meals are fairly expensive, but offerings include pigeon meat and a range of seafood dishes.

Pizzeria les Coupoles

☎ 05 5308 2297

Nicely situated in the alleyways of the Galeries Daumesnil. Périgord is a carnivore's delight but hardly a paradise for vegetarians. However, Les Coupoles offers vegetarians, as well as carnivores, the chance to eat well in attractive surroundings.

Shopping

Périgueux has a wide range of shops, including chain stores and specialist shops. There is ample opportunity to buy souvenirs, excellent local products and produce. Good shopping streets include the Rue Taillefer and theRue Limogeanne. There is a fruit and vegetable market in the Place du Coderc and the all the street markets offer wonderful value and great entertainment.

Market Days

Wednesday and Saturday, with night markets on Wednesday.

Supermarkets

There is a Leclerc supermarket at Trellisac, on the Limoges road, and a Carrefour store in the big out-of-town commercial centre at Boulazac, where the Brive and Limoges roads meet.

Tourist Information Centre

Office du Tourisme

☎ 05 5353 1063

26 Place Francheville

3. The White Périgord

Périgueux is the base town for our Touch of Venice Tour. As we have seen, Paul Abadie rebuilt Périgueux's cathedral in a style reminiscent of St Mark's in Venice, but there is a further touch of Venice 17 miles (27km) to the north of the regional capital, at Brantôme. This little town, with its many bridges over the River Dronne, has the unofficial title of the 'Venice of Périgord' and is a wonderful place for 'messing about on the river'. However, it is not simply the watery setting that gives Brantôme its charm; the town is full of attractive buildings with fine architectural details. Its pleasant park and waterside paths make it a perfect place in which to take an afternoon stroll. Brantôme is one of my favourite Périgord towns.

Our short tour (ideal for a day out) also includes a drive along the very pretty Dronne Valley, a visit to the highly picturesque village of Bourdeilles, a diversion to see the amazing carvings on the church of Grand–Brassac, and a surprise encounter with a large abbey and a beautiful small Romanesque church at Chancelade.

Much of the White Périgord is characterised by broad valleys with extensive limestone ridges and chalky outcrops, but there is a large area to the west of Périgueux that contains a very different type of scenery; here the land is much flatter and largely covered by an extensive forest known as the **Forêt de la Double**. I do not find the Double a particularly appealing region: the buildings are not nearly as attractive as

Top Tips

The Touch of Venice Tour

Not to be missed

- The town of Brantôme
- Brantôme Abbey
- Troglodyte tour at Brantôme
- Drive along the tourist route from Brantôme to Bourdeilles
- Village and castle at Bourdeilles
- Church at Grand-Brassac
- Chapel of St-Jean, Chancelade
- Abbey at Chancelade

Things to do

- Have a meal at a restaurant in Brantôme
- Wander around the Tuesday & Friday markets at Brantôme
- Buy dinosaur footprints or other fossils in Brantôme
- Wander by the river in Brantôme
- Watch canoeists shooting the rapids in Brantôme
- Shoot the rapids yourself in Brantôme, by hiring a canoe
- Take a cruise on the Dronne at Brantôme
- Hire a pedal-car at Brantôme
- Hire a horse-drawn barge at Brantôme
- Go riding at Brantôme or Bourdeilles
- Go canoeing at Bourdeilles
- Have a romantic weekend at Bourdeilles

those in the rest of the Dordogne and the small villages have a run-down feel about them. However, a tour of the area, which is essentially an alternative loop from Périgueux to Brantôme, is included, because there is a developing recreation and water sports centre in the heart of the forest, at the Grand-Étang de la Jemaye, and the journey does take in a château with important Canadian connections and an interesting Trappist monastery.

THE TOUCH OF VENICE TOUR

From Périgueux, we follow signs for Angoulême and then take the D939 for Brantôme.

The road soon passes through the village of **Château-l'Évêque**. This is not a particularly attractive settlement, but the impressive episcopal castle dominates the northern exit from the village in a very satisfying way. The D939 then heads for Brantôme.

The approach to Brantôme gives little indication of the charming scenes which the town has in store for us; the houses, built of large limestone blocks, are rather severe and somewhat shabby and our first encounter with the town centre is a confrontation with the vast slab-like wall of the abbey, but as soon as we park (for free) in the little market place and leave our vehicle, we will discover the easy charm of this riverside town.

BRANTÔME

Part of Brantôme is built on an island in the River Dronne and this area is linked to the rest of the town by five bridges. Brantôme is a very satisfying whole, but also contains some delightful set-pieces. One bank of the river is flanked by a low balustraded wall, behind which are galleried houses clothed in Virginia creeper. This part of the river-bank is a photographer's dream and also a gourmet's delight, as the Fil d'Eau restaurant is situated here in a perfect setting.

Across the river, there is a park which contains a nice architectural surprise: a modest little sheltered seating area whose roof is supported by the grandest of Corinthian columns. At the end of the park there is a sixteenth century 'elbow' bridge (it has a bend in the middle) which leads to the incredibly picturesque **Moulin de l'Abbaye**, with its working water-wheel and its very high quality accommodation and restaurant. Next to the mill there is an exquisite **Renaissance Pavilion**, which now houses the Information Centre (*syndicat d'initiative*).

The convent buildings now house the Town Hall, as well as the **Musée Fernand-Desmoulin**, an art gallery with works by what I would call 'second division' artists.

The bank of the Dronne to the right of the pavilion is completely dominated by **Brantôme Abbey**, founded by Charlemagne in 769, to house the relics of St Sicaire, one of Herod's slaves who was converted to Christianity after the Massacre of the Holy Innocents. Major rebuilding work has been carried out at regular intervals, in the eleventh, sixteenth, eighteenth and nineteenth centuries. The convent buildings have a long, boring white façade, but the church, at the far end of the convent, has a wonderful, four-storey detached **belfry**. This superbly proportioned structure is the oldest bell-tower in France. The church features a stone relief of the Massacre of the Holy Innocents, testimony to its former status as a pilrimage centre dedicated to St Sicaire.

The abbey stands at the foot of a long ridge, thickly wooded in its higher reaches, but riddled with caves and troglodyte dwellings in its lower

The Abbot and the Amorous Ladies

Bourdeilles was one of the four baronies of Périgord, the others being Beynac, Biron and Maureuil. Legend has it that the Bourdeilles family became famous for their ability to slay griffons (hence the name of the hostelry at Bourdeilles).

Pierre de Bourdeilles was born at the château of Bourdeilles in 1540. He became the lay abbot of the abbey at Brantôme but also a soldier of fortune, fighting in various parts of Europe and in Africa. In addition, he acted as a courtier to Mary Queen of Scots during her imprisonment at Leith.

In the course of his travels and through his diverse activities, Pierre de Bourdeilles got to know many leading soldiers, statesmen and members of the court. He used this knowledge to good effect by writing a series of frank and racy biographies of the famous. After becoming crippled as a result of a fall from his horse, he retired to the abbey at Brantôme, assumed the name of the town as a nom-de-plume, and completed his biographical chronicles.

Not surprisingly, Brantôme's works, *The Lives of Illustrious Men and Great Commanders* and the particularly scandalous *Lives of Amorous Ladies,* were published posthumously.

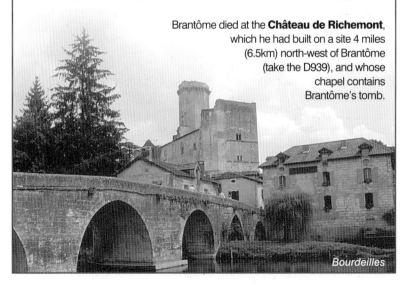

Brantôme died at the **Château de Richemont**, which he had built on a site 4 miles (6.5km) north-west of Brantôme (take the D939), and whose chapel contains Brantôme's tomb.

Bourdeilles

section. The monks used the caves as storerooms, wine-making cellars and also as hide-outs when attack threatened. Guided tours of the caves are available and include the Cave of the Last Judgement, which is decorated with remarkable rock sculptures, a troglodyte dovecote and the Fountain of the Rock, which supposedly has the power to heal infant diseases.

The river is a focus for leisure activities (see below), but it is not simply the water that provides opportunities for healthy outdoor pursuits: pedal cars can be hired for a trip around the town; the GR36 and GR436 walking routes are nearby; and there is an equestrian centre at Les Écuries du Puynadol.

Brantôme is a perfect place for a meal: the quality of the food is excellent and the location is idyllic. There are very good hotels in and around the town and there are two nearby campsites.

River activities

The river at Brantôme is full of activity. Between 1st May and 30th September, a glass-topped boat takes visitors on a leisurely cruise, and canoes can be hired at two centres. Canoeing on the Dronne is a highly popular activity, not least because the weir across the river offers an exciting, but safe challenge to novice canoeists. Most people resort to rocking their boat over the weir, but some find they have to get out of their vessel to tip it over the weir's edge. 'Shooting the rapids' at Brantôme not only provides  the canoeists with great fun and some embarrassing moments, but also keeps the riverside spectators greatly amused. Horse-drawn barges can be hired at Brantôme and there are water jousting tournaments on the Dronne (details from the *syndicat d'initiative*).

Shooting the rapids, Brantôme

Opposite page: Mill and Renaissance Château, Bourdeilles

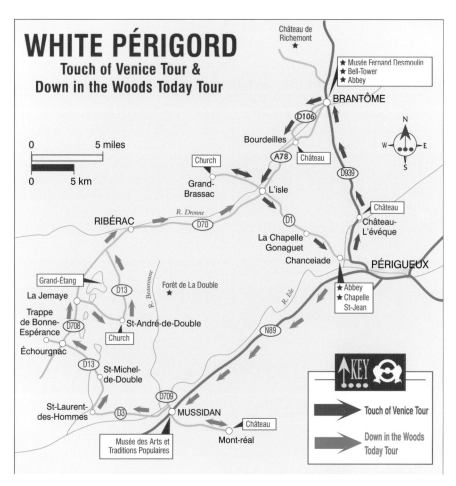

WHITE PÉRIGORD
Touch of Venice Tour &
Down in the Woods Today Tour

Château de Richemont
★

★ Musée Fernand Desmoulin
★ Bell-Tower
★ Abbey

BRANTÔME

D106

Bourdeilles

A78   Château

Church

Grand-Brassac

L'isle

D939

0   5 miles

0   5 km

R. Dronne

RIBÉRAC

D70

D1

Château

Château-L'évêque

La Chapelle Gonaguet

Chanceiade

PÉRIGUEUX

N
W   E
S

Grand-Étang

R. Beauronne

Forêt de La Double
★

R. Isle

★ Abbey
★ Chapelle St-Jean

La Jemaye

D13

Trappe de Bonne-Espérance

D708

St-André-de-Double

Church

N89

Échourgnac

D13

St-Michel-de-Double

D709

St-Laurent-des-Hommes

D3

MUSSIDAN

Château

KEY

Touch of Venice Tour

Musée des Arts et Traditions Populaires

Mont-réal

Down in the Woods Today Tour

Shopping

On a slightly less energetic note, shopping in Brantôme is a pleasurable activity. On the occasion of my last visit, the main pedestrianised shopping street (*rue piétonne*) was decked out with plastic and paper bunting. One shop sells the most spectacular fossils and stones, including dinosaur prints. The ice cream on sale by the market place is delicious; there are traditional farm markets on Tuesdays in July and August; there is a winter truffle market and even a European Bread Festival.

ON TO BOURDEILLES

From Brantôme, we take the D106 tourist route along the River Dronne, past overhanging limestone cliffs on our right and soft meadowland on our left. This beautiful green and white landscape is punctuated by brilliant splashes of golden yellow sunflower fields.

After a sublime journey of 6 miles (9.7km), we arrive at the picture postcard village of **Bourdeilles** (illustrated on pages 61,62). A thirteenth century humped bridge, with a succession of packhorse refuges on one side only, leads to the village. The sixteenth century Hostellerie des Griffons, a delightful hotel and restaurant ideal for a romantic weekend, is on our right. An old mill and a great castle is on our left. The huge and austere walls of the old fortress are softened by an adjacent

Renaissance château which was added to the castle in the fifteenth century. The château contains the sumptuous Golden Room which was built for Catherine de Medici who had promised to make a visit to the castle. She never came! The Golden Room contains an elaborate chimney piece, a painted ceiling and a superb tapestry. From the upper rooms, there is a magnificent view over the lovely valley of the Dronne.

Canoes can be hired at Canoës Bourdeilles and there is an equestrian centre at the Ferme Équestre le Naudonnet.

L'ISLE TO PÉRIGUEUX

We leave Bourdeilles by the D78 for **L'Isle**, where there is a nice picnic area by the river and a playground which includes a slide that tips children into the River Isle. A right turn at L'Isle takes us up a long, winding road to the village of **Grand-Brassac** where there is a rather special church.

The north doorway of the church is topped by a group of five statuettes, representing Christ, the Virgin, St John, St Peter and St Paul. These stand on the arch of an elaborate Romanesque portal, within which are further statuettes representing the Adoration of the Magi. The interior of the church is plain, as is usual in the Dordogne region, but on my most recent visit I found it decked out with vases of highly fragrant flowers.

The modest little village of Grand-Brassac is unusual in having a number of houses with rather pretentious balustrades.

The long and the short of it

The three skeletons found in the Cro-Magnon cave near Les Eyzies during the construction of a railway embankment in 1868 were important discoveries for prehistorians. Cro-Magnon man, who lived in the Dordogne region over 30,000 years ago, had an upright posture and a brain capacity similar to modern man. He was commonly about 6ft (1.8m) tall.

The skeleton discovered at Chancelade in 1888 is only some 15,000 years old. Chancelade man also had a large brain capacity but he had a broad face with high cheekbones and he was only some 5ft 2ins (1.58m) in height.

Some experts believe that he was a member of a race of reindeer hunters who eventually left the Dordogne and moved north with the reindeer when the climate warmed up.

If we now retrace our route to L'Isle, we can pick up the D1 for Périgueux. This road runs through a very green and pleasant land and passes through a surprising little place called **La-Chapelle-Gonaguet** which has houses with rather incongruous red-tiled roofs. There is also a Romanesque chapel in the village.

Just as we seem to be approaching the suburbs of Périgueux and the end of our journey, we come across another surprise. In a peaceful hollow to our left, lies the exquisite Romanesque **Chapelle St-Jean** with an exterior which, to my eyes, is perfect in both form and detail. As we have come to expect in Dordogne churches, the interior is very bare and plain.

In the green valley below the chapel, there is the large **Abbaye de Chancelade**, built on the site of a twelfth century Augustine priory. The original abbey was captured by the English in the Hundred Years' War, briefly recovered by du Guesclin, recaptured by the English, and later destroyed by the Protestants in the Wars of Religion. The abbey became national property during the Revolution.

The bell-tower and doorway of the abbey church are both Romanesque and the choir stalls are seventeenth century and fashioned in walnut. The convent has stables, workshops, a mill and an abbot's residence.

It is now a short journey back to Périgueux.

TOUR 2: DOWN IN THE WOODS TODAY

an alternative loop fromPérigueux to Brantôme

Grand Étang de la Jemaye

Top Tips

Down in the Woods Today Tour

Not to be missed

- Château and chapel at Mont-Réal
- Prettiest house in the Double at St Laurent-des-Hommes
- Trappe de Bonne-Espérance monastery
- Grand Étang de la Jemaye
- Church at St-André-de-Double

Things to do

- Walk from Périgueux to St-Laurent-des-Hommes along the GR646
- Buy cheeese at the Trappe de Bonne-Espérance
- Picnic at the Grand Étang de la Jemaye
- Hire a paddle boat or a canoe or water skis at the Grand Étang de la Jemaye
- Go riding or pony trekking in the Double
- Shop at the Friday market at Ribérac

As I mentioned in the introduction to this chapter, I do not find a large part of this alternative route scenically attractive, but it is included because there are several points of interest and also opportunities, at the Étang de la Jamaye, for outdoor pursuits and watersports.

We leave Périgueux on the N89 for **Mussidan**. Our route takes us through limestone country, evidenced by the rocky outcrops and the simple houses fashioned in white stone. The villages in this region are rather hard and plain in appearance, in marked contrast with the stone-built villages along the Dordogne and Vézère valleys where the buildings have a much richer and softer feel.

MUSSIDAN

Mussidan is one of those towns which is described in guide books as 'industrial' or 'not particularly attractive', guidebook euphemism for 'ugly'. However, Mussidan does have the **Musée des Arts et Traditions Populaires,** a museum

Above: Abbaye de Bonne-Espérance

Right: Woods of the Double

containing an interesting collection of furniture, machinery and tools, and mock-ups of nineteenth century rooms and workshops. We turn left at Mussidan along the D36 for the hill known as **Mont-Réal**, a place of particular interest to visitors from the New World. At the summit, we find the **Château de Mont-Réal,** surrounded by ramparts and a now waterless moat.

A chapel, built within the grounds of the château by François de Pont-briand, contains the Holy Thorn, supposedly a thorn from the Crown of Thorns, which was carried by Sir John Talbot when he died at the Battle of Castillon in 1453. Montreal in Canada was given its name by Claude de Pontbriand who accompanied Jacques Cartier on his second expedition up the St Lawrence river in 1535.

On my last visit to the Dordogne, I made the diversion from Mussidan to Mont-Réal after being seduced by a stunningly beautiful photograph of the chapel which I had seen in a book. Unfortunately, I arrived at lunchtime when the chapel was closed, and my schedule would not allow a return trip. My disappointment was immense and, for the time being, I shall have to rely on reports from readers to discover whether the chapel really is as beautiful as photographs suggest. Do let me know!

MUSSIDAN TO GRAND ÉTANG DE LA JEMAYE

After returning to Mussidan, we cross over the N89 and follow the D709, signposted Ribérac, but then take a left turn on the D3 to St-Laurent and the Forêt de la Double. The villages and hamlets which we pass through have a run-down, 'one-horse town' feel about them, but at St-Laurent itself, properly called **St-Laurent-des-Hommes**, we come across a seventeenth century, balconied, half-timbered house, which has the reputation of being the 'prettiest house in the Double'. If truth be known, the building has very little competition in the beauty stakes in this region!

The GR646 runs through St-Laurent and there is a splendid walking route from here to Périgueux. Horse riding is available at the equestrian centre Beauperier.

We now take the D13 to **St-Michel-de-Double** and then go on to **Échourgnac** where we go straight across the D708 in order to reach the **Trappe de Bonne Espérance**, a monastery founded in 1868 by Trappist monks from Normandy.

The monks left the monastery in 1910, but were replaced in 1923 by Trappist nuns. The monks had established a renowned cheese-making plant here and the nuns have carried on the industry. There is a nice display area and gift shop in the grounds of the monastery where cheese and other souvenirs can be purchased. The shop is closed on Mondays. Those people who really want to 'get away from it all' can even go into retreat here by booking a place in one of a score of guestrooms at the monastery.

We now return to the D708 and the road for the **Grand Étang de la Jemaye**, a large lake at the heart of the forest. The shores of the lake make an ideal picnic spot under the shade of the trees. There are rudimentary open-air cafés and stalls selling chips, pizzas, and the like. It is possible to hire canoes, paddle boats and water skis, or simply swim or go for a paddle in the lake. The forest is very inviting too, and horse riding and pony trekking are available for visitors.

All-in-all, this is a very pleasant place

indeed and ideal for a host of outdoor activities, be they land or water based, but the facilities here have not been developed as much as one would have imagined. Normally, I would applaud this state of affairs, finding it far preferable to the vast marinas and theme parks which disfigure so many beauty spots, but the Grand-Étang has that run-down or more accurately, in this case, not-fully-developed feel, which pervades so much of the Double.

Back to L'Isle

The road now leads to **St-André-de-Double**, where there is an imposing speckled-sandstone church that stands on a sort of dais. However, St-André is yet another example of a run-down Double village, more ghost town than 'one-horse town'. In fact, I almost jumped out of my skin on my last visit when I heard voices coming from inside a building which looked far too dilapidated to sustain human habitation.

We follow the D708 to **Ribérac**. A very extensive street market is held throughout the town on Fridays, but there is little else to detain us here. The D710 takes us along the pleasant Dronne valley towards L'Isle, where we can head back to either Brantôme or Périgueux.

Double Trouble

The region known as the Double lies between the River Dronne and the River Isle. Forests of chestnut and oak have covered much of this region for centuries and sixty per cent of the area is still under forest.

Stone is scarce in the Double so the traditional building material was timber until the advent of modern synthetic building materials. Very few old timber-framed houses remain, although an effort has been made to revive the style in some of the newest properties.

Until the nineteenth century, when the Trappist monks set up home at the Monastery of Bonne-Espérance and drained and cultivated some of the area, the Double was regarded as a hostile and desolate place. The marshes and bogs were breeding grounds for malarial mosquitoes, the clay soils made cultivation difficult, and the woods provided a home for wolves and wild boar. The resident peasants had a hard life and most other people, apart from criminals seeking refuge from justice, avoided the place completely.

Timber prouction, a little dairy farming and some recreational provision (at the Grand Étang de la Jemaye) are the chief activities in the Double today, but the region still has a desolate air about it. Tourists looking for attractive villages and archetypal French ambience would do well to avoid the place.

Additional Information

The White Périgord

Accommodation

Hôtels

There are some very high class (and expensive) hotels in picturesque settings in both Brantôme and Bourdeilles, plus some cheaper, but perfectly acceptable alternatives:

Bourdeilles
Les Griffons *
☎ 05 5303 7561
10 rooms, idyllic setting.

Les Tilleuls-Tourisme
☎ 05 5303 7640
6 rooms.

Brantôme
Hôtel Chabrol *
☎ 05 5305 7015 19 rooms.

Le Châtenet *
☎ 05 5305 8108

Domaine de la Roseraie *
☎ 05 5305 8474
10 rooms, swimming pool.

Moulin de l'Abbaye *
☎ 05 5305 8022
19 rooms, good restaurant.

Hostellerie du Périgord Vert **
☎ 05 5305 7058
16 rooms.

Hôtel Aliénor **
☎ 05 5305 8536

Chancelade
Château des Reynats Hôtel **
☎ 05 5303 5359
37 rooms, swimming pool, tennis.

Étang des Reynats **
☎ 05 5354 7958
20 rooms, swimming pool, tennis.

Below: Pavilion and weir, Brantôme

Above: Pleasure boat trip on the river, Brantôme

Le Pont de la Beauronne *
☎ 05 5308 4291
28 rooms.

L'Isle
Le Sans Souci **
☎ 05 5304 5836
9 rooms.

Mussidan
Hôtel du Midi **
☎ 05 5381 0177
9 rooms, swimming pool.

Les Voyageurs *
☎ 05 5381 0012.

Hôtel du Grand Café-Tourisme
☎ 05 5381 0007
10 rooms.

Ribérac
Hôtel de France **
☎ 05 5390 0061
16 rooms.

**** Rev' Hôtel**
☎ 05 5391 6262. 17 rooms.

Hôtel de l'Univers-Tourisme
☎ 05 5390 0438. 10 rooms.

Campsites

The area covered in these tours is well served by campsites:
For camping Le Grand Dague, see the chapter on Périgueux.

Brantôme
Camping Peyrelevade **
☎ 05 5305 7524
Municipal site, 170 emplacements

Les Écuries de Puynadal *
☎ 05 5306 1966
30 emplacements, swimming pool.

Échourgnac
Les Chaumes *
☎ 05 5380 3656
Municipal site, 40 emplacements, tennis.

Additional Information

L'Isle
Camping le Pont ★★
☎ 05 5354 5881
45 emplacements, tennis.

La Jemaye
Grand Étang ★
☎ 05 5390 1851
33 emplacements.

Mussidan
Le Port ★
☎ 05 5381 2009
Municipal site, 25 emplacements, swimming pool.

Ribérac
La Dronne ★★
☎ 05 5390 5008
Municipal site, 100 emplacements.

Activity Centres
Bourdeilles
Canoeing
Canoës Bourdeilles
☎ 05 5304 5694

Horse Riding
Ferme Équestre le Naudonnet
☎ 05 5308 6674

Brantôme
Boat Trips
Le Pont Coude
☎ 05 5305 7724

Canoeing
☎ 05 5305 7724

Allo Canoë Brantôme Canoë
☎ 05 5306 3185

Horse Riding
Les Écuries du Puynadal
☎ 05 5306 1966

Attractions
Bourdeilles
Château
☎ 05 5303 7336
Open: daily 10am–7pm Jul to early Sep; 10am–12 noon, 2–6pm Apr to Jun and early Sep to mid-Oct, closed Tue 2–5pm; 2–5pm at other times of year; closed Tue and Christmas Day.

Brantôme
Abbey and Troglodyte Tour
☎ 05 5305 8063
Open: 10am–12 noon, 2–6pm; closed Tue Sep to Jun.

Bell-tower
☎ 05 5305 8165
Guided tours available in the afternoons from mid-Jun to mid-Sep.

Château de Richemont
☎ 05 5305 7281
Open: 10am–12 noon, 3–6pm mid-Jul to end of Aug; closed Fri, Sun am and Aug 15th.

Musée Fernand-Desmoulin
☎ 05 5305 7021
Open: 10am–12 noon, 2–6pm; closed Tue.

Chancelade
Abbey
☎ 05 5304 8687
Open: daily 2–7pm July and August.

Mont-Réal
Château and Chapel
☎ 05 5381 2094
Open: 10am–12 noon, 2–6pm 1st Jul to 30th Sep.

Mussidan
Musée des Arts et Traditions Populaires
☎ 05 5381 2355
Open: 9.30am–12 noon, 2–6pm Jun to mid-Sep, closed Tue; 2–6pm Sat, Sun and holidays out of season.

Eating Out

Not surprisingly, this area of Périgord contains restaurants in superb riverside locations. The eating places in Bourdeilles and Brantôme are ideal spots for a romantic evening.

Bourdeilles
Les Griffons
☎ 05 5345 4535
Occupies a wonderful spot at the foot of the castle. The restaurant is on a terrace by the river.

Brantôme
Au Fil de l'Eau
☎ 05 5305 7365
Has a superb riverside dining room and good food at surprisingly reasonable prices.

Le Moulin de l'Abbaye
☎ 05 5305 8022
Also occupies a superb riverside location by the picturesque Elbow Bridge. This is one of Périgord's finest restaurants, with prices to match its status.

Le Vieux Four
☎ 05 5305 7416
Offers something a little different. This is the place to eat if you are a pizza fan.

Ribérac
Hôtel de France
☎ 05 5390 0062
Has a good restaurant which serves traditional dishes. You could call in here after a drive through the Double.

Shopping

There is ample opportunity for shopping, especially for souvenirs, in Brantôme. The markets at Brantôme and Ribérac are excellent.

Market Days

Brantôme – Friday (plus Tuesday in July, August)

Ribérac – Friday

Supermarkets

There are Leclerc and Intermarché supermarkets at St Astier, mid-way between Périgueux and Mussidan.

There is a Leclerc supermarket at Ribérac and an Intermarché at Mussidan.

Syndicats d'Initiative

Bourdeilles	☎ 05 5303 4296
Brantôme	☎ 05 5305 8052
Mussidan	☎ 05 5381 7387

Tourist Information Centre

Ribérac	☎ 05 5390 0310

4. The Purple Périgord

The south-west region of the Dordogne is now known as the Purple Périgord (*Périgord Pourpre*). This is the land of the *bastides*, medieval towns constructed on a grid plan around a central square and market place.

Many of Europe's best preserved medieval settlements have become favoured places of residence for commuters, others have become little more than weekend retreats for city-dwellers, whilst others have become art and craft villages. All of these changes are to be applauded because they have extended the life of places whose original function is largely obsolete and they have allowed the continent's rich medieval architectural legacy to survive into the twenty-first century. However, the character of many villages has changed beyond recognition, because the cosmetic operations carried out on them have been so extensive. The *bastides* of the Purple Périgord have not suffered this fate; they remain working market towns in the heart of the countryside and they offer visiting tourists a genuine opportunity to step back in time.

The Purple Périgord is an intoxicating area, but much of the landscape lacks the heady drama of the central Dordogne region. You will not find

Wine country

The Purple Périgord takes its name from the colour of the grapes that produce some of France's most famous wines, the full-bodied reds of Bergerac and the sweet white Monbazillacs. As we have learnt, much of the Dordogne's wine industry was destroyed when disease crippled the vines, but extensive vineyards still stretch over the slopes to the south of Bergerac. Our journey takes us to a wine château which is every bit as idyllic in appearance as any picture you are likely to see on the label of a wine bottle.

narrow gorges and overhanging cliffs in most of this part of Périgord; much of the countryside is open and gently undulating, and the fertile soil supports large fields of maize, tobacco and sunflowers. But the first part of our journey does take us past a spectacular loop in the Dordogne river and through one of Périgord's most beautiful clinging villages, which also happens to be one of the best locations for embarking on a canoe trip. We also visit a famous abbey and a massive hilltop château, and we have a very special treat in store for film buffs!

The town of **Le Bugue** is not strictly part of the Purple Périgord, but it has been chosen as our base because it has ample accommodation, including a superbly equipped holiday centre and caravan and camping site, and it is a centrally located cross–roads town that gives easy access to all parts of the Dordogne.

Above: Entry to the Old Town, Limeuil

TOUR 1: LE BUGUE
& THE BASTIDES

LE BUGUE

Le Bugue sits on the north bank of the Vézère river. As the signpost on the crossroads at the heart of the town indicates, roads from all areas of the Dordogne meet here. The town is not particularly attractive, but it does have a partially renovated Old Town area, a picturesque bridge over the Vézère, a nice lake and fountain by the church, and a plethora of wrought-iron balconies, evidence of a once thriving local iron industry.

There is plenty of accommodation in the town, including the 3-star Royal Vézère, nicely situated by the river. The hotel has a private swimming pool and its pavement café is a pleasant location for an evening drink. St-Avit-Loisirs, deep in the woods, just 3.5 miles (6km) to the west of the town, is an extensive holiday complex. The site has a large number of *emplacements* for caravans and tents, and there are holiday bungalows to let. Sporting facilities include tennis, volleyball, archery and cycle hire; there are superb indoor and outdoor swimming pools; there is a children's club, an on-site restaurant and nightly entertainment.

Le Bugue attractions:

The **Aquarium du Périgord Noir** attracts a large number of visitors, but there is free parking for 300 cars. Facilities include a picnic area, food and drink bar, souvenir shop, and particularly good access for disabled people. The path through the exhibition runs through a well-lit tunnel below a glass-bottomed aquarium and past glass-walled aquaria on either side. Visitors are made to feel as if they have dived underwater to view the fish.

There are two show caves in the vicinity: **Grotte de Bara-Bahau**, 1.2 miles (2km) to the north-west of the town, which contains cave drawings of bears, as well as some rather more indecipherable marks; the **Gouffre de Proumeyssac**, 2 miles (3km) south of Le Bugue, which contains a domed chamber with yellow and white stalactites hanging from the roof like crystal. Both caves are open daily.

Le Bournat, just east of Le Bugue, is a reconstructed village which tries to recreate life in the Dordogne at the end of the nineteenth century. There are steam engines, small farms, a school, and lots of workshops with frequent demonstrations by local craftsmen and women.

The GR6, which also links up with the GR36 and GR461, provides wonderful opportunities for walks in some of the Dordogne's finest landscapes. Canoes can be hired at Les Courrèges for a trip along the Vézère.

On most evenings, it is possible to watch the locals, or even join in with them, as they play boules, and on Tuesdays and Saturdays there is a thriving local market. The town's extensive graveyard is interesting in a more macabre way. In common with most French burial grounds, it contains large, elaborate tombs decorated with ornate tributes and mementoes.

Top Tips

Tour 1: The Bastides

Not to be missed

- **Aquarium du Périgord Noir**, Le Bugue
- **Grotte de Bara-Bahau**
- **Gouffre de Proumeyssac**
- **Le Bournat** nineteenth century village
- **Birdland**, Le Bugue
- **Chapelle St-Martin**
- **Limeuil village**
- The **view of the Dordogne near Trémolat**
- The location for **Le Boucher at Trémolat**
- **Lanquais château**
- **Beaumont church**
- **Biron château**
- **Villeréal market hall**
- The Square at **Monpazier**
- Old houses, **Issigeac**

Things to do

- Watch the world go by in the pavement café at Le Bugue's Royal Vézère
- Join in a game of boules, Le Bugue
- Walk on the GR36 and GR6 paths
- Hire a canoe at Le Bugue
- Visit Le Bugue's cemetery
- Play golf at Golf de Croix de Morlemart, Le Bugue
- Photograph sunflowers
- Canoe down the Vézère or Dordogne from Limeuil
- Visit the Thursday market at Lalinde
- Join a paper-making class at Couze-et-St-Front
- Picnic outside the walls of Lanquais château
- Visit the fair on the second Tuesday of the month at Beaumont
- Visit the fair on the third Thursday of the month at Monpazier
- Photograph or sketch half-timbered houses at Issigeac
- If you have not brought your cycle, hire one at Monpazier, Trémolat or Bergerac

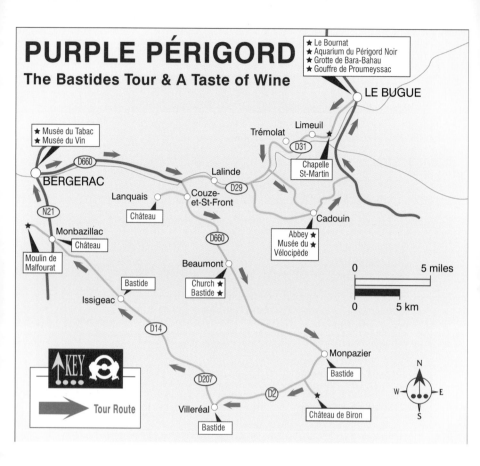

PURPLE PÉRIGORD
The Bastides Tour & A Taste of Wine

★ Le Bournat
★ Aquarium du Périgord Noir
★ Grotte de Bara-Bahau
★ Gouffre de Proumeyssac

LE BUGUE

★ Musée du Tabac
★ Musée du Vin

Trémolat   Limeuil

D31

D660   Lalinde   Chapelle St-Martin

BERGERAC

Lanquais   Couze-et-St-Front   D29

N21   Château

Château   Cadouin

Monbazillac   Abbey ★
Château   Musée du ★ Vélocipède
Moulin de Malfourat   D660

Beaumont   0   5 miles

Bastide   Church ★
Bastide ★   0   5 km

Issigeac

D14

KEY

Monpazier

Tour Route   Bastide   N

D207   W   E

D2   S

Villeréal

Bastide   Château de Biron

A splash of yellow

For British tourists travelling into France from the Channel ports, the first sighting of a field of golden yellow sunflowers marks the entrance to the hot and sunny south. The huge fields look like a great splash of yellow pigment which has been spilt accidentally from an enormous paint pot.

Van Gogh turned this highly evocative flower, which opens up in the heat of the day in vivid imitation of the sun, into an icon. The yellow fields of oil seed rape which are increasingly intruding into the English countryside seem literally to rape our green and pleasant land, but the yellow colour of the sunflower appears to be an altogether appropriate element in the sunny landscapes of southern France.

Sunflowers were once used as animal feed but they are now harvested to produce a light cooking oil.

Above: View of the Dordogne, from the road to Trémolat

Right: The riverside, Limeuil

Below: Wedding car, Lanquais

THE BASTIDES

We leave Le Bugue by the D703 and then take the D31 towards Limeuil. Our first spectacular encounter is with the **Chapelle St-Martin**, which stands in splendid isolation in the fields on our left. The construction of this beautiful domed chapel, fashioned in the gorgeous local golden stone, is said to have been funded by Henry II as penance for the death of St Thomas Becket. Richard the Lionheart, whose name appears on the foundation stone in the nave, sponsored the completion of the building in 1194.

Immediately beyond the chapel, there are huge fields of golden yellow sunflowers. The temptation to stop and take photographs is too great to resist. The road then drops down to **Limeuil** and the confluence of the Dordogne and Vézère rivers. We can park for free on the riverbank and savour the beauty of this wonderful spot.

LIMEUIL

Limeuil is the perfect place for hiring a canoe. It is possible to make a gentle 4.5-mile (7km) trip along the Vézère to Le Bugue or a more demanding 18-mile (29km) journey to La Roque-St-Christophe. The Dordogne river provides lots of opportunities, including a 20-mile (32km) trip to Beynac and a leisurely 3.5-mile (6km) cruise in the opposite direction to Trémolat. A return minibus service for canoeists operates along the riverside roads. There are stops at regular intervals.

There is an open-air café on the shore with splendid views of the two rivers and their identical bridges. Across the road, there are displays of work by local artists. Amateur painters and lesser known artists in France seem to put a great deal of effort into developing a unique personal style, sometimes at the expense of quality and interesting subject matter, but the paintings on display at Limeuil are both distinctive and appealing.

The village of Limeuil is entered through an arched gateway. The settlement, which clings to a bluff above the confluence, is constructed from the golden stone of the locality. Given its strategic position, it is not surprising to learn that it was an important fortified town in the Middle Ages. Three town gates and a fragment of wall survive, and there is a ruined château above the maze of narrow streets. Limeuil is so enchanting that it is very hard to leave the place.

As we climb the winding road to the west of Limeuil, a superb view of the hill-village appears in our rear-view mirror. At the summit of our road there is a pull-in which affords a fine view over a bend in the Dordogne river. The panorama is extensive.

TRÉMOLAT

The road drops down to the village of **Trémolat**, where the scene is instantly recognisable to anyone who has seen Chabrol's gripping film *Le Boucher*. The village school, the Mairie, the church and a few shops, including a butcher's shop, all front onto the town square. The scene is so strangely quiet and eerie (at least it was on my visit) that one almost expects the village schoolmistress and the murderous butcher who appeared in the classic film to appear on the scene.

The interior of the twelfth century fortified church has crumbled so much that it has to be supported by scaffolding, which was cleverly camouflaged by a covering of flowers at the time of my visit. A side road to the north of the town leads to another spectacular view over the meandering Dordogne.

ON TO COUZE-ET-ST-FRONT

We now take the D31 to **Lalinde**, where we cross the Dordogne via the D29. Lalinde is a busy little town which has a very extensive Thursday market. The town's street plan betrays its origin as a thirteenth century *bastide*, founded by Edward III of England.

After taking the D703 towards Bergerac, we cross the Dordogne once again for **Couze-et-St-Front**, where we take a right turn along the D37 for the **Château de Lanquais**. The road up to the castle is very rough and a severe test for the suspension of both vehicle and passengers, but the rewards at the summit are immense. Outside the castle walls, there are nice shady spots where it is possible to park and enjoy a picnic.

We can now return to Couze-et-St-Front (where it is possible to attend paper-making courses in the summer months) and pick up the D660 for **Beaumont**, the first in a string of remarkably well-preserved *bastides* on our itinerary.

BEAUMONT

Beaumont was founded in 1272 by Lucas de Thanay, a lieutenant of Edward I of England. One of the town's fortified gates, the Porte de Luzier, has not only survived to the present day, but also retains the grooves which mark the position of its portcullis. There is also a fragment of the original town wall and the streets of Beaumont have the grid pattern which is characteristic of *bastide* towns. All *bastides* were granted a market charter and they were all constructed with a large central square and market area. Some of the houses which surround Beaumont's square are arcaded.

By far the most dominant feature of Beaumont is the massive fortified church, the last refuge of the townspeople against attackers. The defensive purpose of the building is evidenced by its austere walls, its towers, its ramparts and its parapet for archers. The west front has a rather more ecclesiastical aspect: there is a decorated frieze which carries carvings depicting the four Evangelists, a hunt, a siren and a king, who may or may not be Edward I. The interior of the church was greatly modified in the nineteenth century.

The market square, which is the venue for a fair on the second Tuesday of each month, is always a lively place, but it is the massive, brooding presence of the fortified church that leaves a lasting impression.

We can now return to the D660 and drive across quiet, open countryside to **Monpazier**, the most famous *bastide* of them all.

Périgord's Old 'New Towns'

Bastides are identified at their boundaries by a signpost that carries a distinctive geometric design reflecting the rectangular shape and grid-like street pattern of all such towns. *Bastides* normally have defensive curtain walls and gateways and a good number of them even have fortified churches. Although they were clearly constructed with defence in mind, they were primarily built to settle uncultivated areas of countryside.

Bastides were founded by both the English and the French. Alphonse de Poitiers was one of the most prolific of *bastides* builders, but a number of these 'new towns' were established by Edward I of England.

All *bastides* were granted a market charter and they all have a large central square and a covered market hall. Many of the houses that surround the square have *couverts*, covered arcades that give shelter from sun and rain to the traders and their customers.

Although all *bastides* have a common geometry and the same architectural ingredients, they differ in emphasis. Each of the *bastides* chosen for our tour leaves its own distinctive impression. The silhouette of Beaumont's immense fortified church lives on in the mind; Monpazier's arcaded square is very memorable; Villeréal's huge timbered market hall is visually impressive and Issigeac's half-timbered houses have picture-postcard appeal.

MONPAZIER

Monpazier is another English *bastide*, founded in 1285 by Edward I. Although the town has been much fought over and has changed hands on a number of occasions, it has survived remarkably well. The fortifications are still very evident; three of the original six gates remain and the precise rectangular geometry of the town and the gridpattern of its streets, which run parallel with the walls and cross each other at right angles, are entirely intact.

As at Beaumont, a fortified church occupies one corner of the market square, but at Monpazier it is the square itself that leaves a lasting impression. Monpazier's square is large and surrounded on three sides by stone-built, arcaded houses, the fourth side being occupied by a covered market hall.

Monpazier is much hyped in travel books and architectural guides and it is undoubtedly a classic among *bastides*. On my first visit to the town, I experienced a very slight feeling of disappointment, perhaps because I found its famous square too empty or too large, or even too perfect! However, on a subsequent visit, I was completely seduced by the place, especially by the market place with its varied but harmonious architecture and its inviting arcades. Tourists seem reluctant to step into the vast open areas of the square, as if they are afraid that they might disturb the perfect picture postcard scene, but

The square at Monpazier

they throng the perimeter arcades, attracted by the fine craft shops and pavement cafés.

The arcades are used as a venue for extensive book fairs and also for village fairs, which are held on the third Thursday of every month. Through an archway in one corner of the square, there is a tantalising glimpse of the very elaborate door-way of Monpazier's church.

One sobering thought before we leave the market place – Buffarot, a leader of the Peasants' Revolt, was broken on the wheel in this square in 1637.

Our tour of the *bastides* is now interrupted by a diversion to **Biron**, seat of one of the four great baronies of Périgord. We travel along the D2 towards Villeréal, but take a left fork when we see signposts for the château.

Our first sight of the castle, which sits massively on the summit of a hill, is very impressive indeed. The present building is the result of many restorations and additions made since a keep was first erected here in the twelfth century. Like many French châteaux, Biron is a mixture of elegant Renaissance house and fortified castle.

The tour begins in the outer courtyard where there are stables, a receiving house, a caretaker's lodge, and also a superb sixteenth century chapel with an upper section containing impressive tombs of noteworthy members of the Biron clan and a lower section which served as a parish church. A staircase and a corridor lead to the Cour d'Honneur, the main courtyard of the castle, where we can walk through galleries that currently house art exhibits and enter the Hall of State with its timbered roof. From the terrace, we can look back across the fields to Monpazier.

Curious to know if our own Lord Byron had any connection with the Périgord Birons, I discovered that he was a distant relative.

VILLERÉAL & ISSIGEAC

By dropping down to the D104, we can take the road to **Villeréal**, yet another *bastide* town. This one was founded in 1269 by Alphonse de Poitiers. The town has the normal *bastide* layout, but its central square is entirely dominated by a massive fourteenth century timbered market hall, supported by scores of wooden pillars. An upper storey was added in the sixteenth century.

By following the D207 and then the D14, we arrive at **Issigeac**, the final *bastide* town on our chosen tour. Issigeac has been described as a picture-postcard town and it has featured in a number of movies, but I have to report that I find the place a little scruffy and somewhat run-down. However, this particular *bastide* is unusual in having a large number of jettied, half-timbered dwellings. There is also a large Bishop's Palace which now houses the town hall.

There are many more *bastides* in Purple Périgord, but we have surely had our fill of grid-patterned, fortified towns for the time being, so we will now proceed to the vineyards of Bergerac for a taste of wine.

The D14 leads to **Monbazillac**. After crossing the N21 and taking a road up to a plateau, we are confronted with a picture taken straight from the label of a wine bottle: a neat, highly picturesque château sitting at the heart of a large vineyard.

Top Tips

Tour 2: Taste of Wine

Not to be missed

- **Château of Monbazillac**
- **Old Town, Bergerac**
- **Wine Museum**, Bergerac
- **Cadouin Abbey**
- **Cycle Museum**, Cadouin

Things to do

- Taste and buy wine at Monbazillac
- Take a ride in a horse-drawn carriage from Monbazillac
- Take refreshment in Bergerac's Old Town
- Take a boat trip on the river at Bergerac

Château de Monbazillac

The Château de Monbazillac, started in 1550 and built of light brown stone, has crenellations running across its façade, round towers at its four corners, and a roofline peppered with dormers and turrets. The interior, which is open to the public, has a Great Hall with a painted ceiling, a massive chimney-piece and Flemish tapestries. The castle also contains a wine museum and a collection of rustic furniture. There is a large shop at the gateway to the vineyard where Monbazillac wine and other Bergerac wines are on sale.

The vineyards, which produce a celebrated sweet white wine, were first planted, as is so often the case, by monks in the eleventh century. The castle is now owned by the Cave Coopérative de Monbazillac which has restored the château to its full glory. It is possible to book a journey in an open-top, horse-drawn cart at the château for a leisurely tour of the wine-producing countryside.

Plonk

I have rarely passed an evening in France without a bottle of wine and a glass close at hand. I know which wines I like and I can easily identify those that are cheap and nasty, but this does not make me a wine connoisseur or even a knowledgeable enthusiast. There are many excellent books and guides to French wine on the market, not least the *Route des Vins de Bergerac* booklet, obtainable from the wine museum in Bergerac. It is also worth noting that most managers of wine departments in French supermarkets are both knowledgeable and helpful. I shall leave it to the experts to dispense detailed advice.

I can report that Monbazillac wines, grown from grapes reared on chalky soil and left on the vine until the autumn, are very sweet and aromatic. The Grande Réserve, Château Monbazillac and Château Septy labels ensure good quality. Montravel wines are less sweet and Bergerac wines can be red, rosé or white. Bergerac Rouge and Pécharmant wines are fruity and full-bodied.

The vineyards of Bergerac have twelve *appellations*: the four red *appellations* are Bergerac Rouge, Côtes de Bergerac, Pécharmant, and Bergerac Rosé; the white *appellations* are Bergerac Sec, Côtes de Bergerac Moelleux, Montravel, Côtes de Montravel Moelleux, Haut Montravel Moelleux, Rosette Moelleux, Saussignac Moelleux and Monbazillac Liquoreux.

Wines from the Bergerac region may not have quite the same reputation as those from the Bordeaux vineyards further west, but the lovely word 'plonk' does at least originate from this region, being a corruption of Planques, the name of a wine château near Bergerac.

Cooling off in the fountain at Bergerac

If we now take a side road up to the **Moulin de Malfourat**, we can enjoy a superb panoramic view across acres of vineyards to the town of **Bergerac**, which can be reached by the D933, the D13 or the N21. All roads lead to Bergerac!

BERGERAC

Bergerac is not the most attractive of towns, although some of the approach roads have been softened by the installation of colourful roadside planters. If we head for the quayside, we can park (for free) on the large cobbled area there and gain easy pedestrian access to the restored Old Town area, which is both picturesque and atmospheric.

The entrance to the Old Town is not very inviting, but we soon find ourselves in an attractive square that rises, Italian style, to a church up

on the hill. Here we find pavement cafés, a nice fountain where we can cool off, a Tourist Information Centre and a **Musée du Vin,** with free access to the wine cellars and the wine shop on the lower floor.

The wine shop has a whole host of free pamphlets and neatly produced information cards containing everything you could wish to know about wine from the Bergerac vineyards. One booklet, called *Route des Vins de Bergerac*, gives a very useful summary of all the wines of the area, be they red, rosé, dry white, sweet white or dessert wines, and lists no less than 105 wine-producing *châteaux*, *domaines* and *caves* in the Bergerac area that are open to the public. Wine connoisseurs will wish to visit a number of these places. **Château de Jaubertie** and **Château de Panisseau** are perhaps the most

A pavement café at Bergerac

tempting, but the very helpful booklet gives clear information on other outlets and their specialities.

Bergerac also has a **Musée du Tabac**, reflecting the other main activity of the area, namely tobacco production. The town has a fair range of shops and stores; there are some good restaurants and several hotels, including the Hôtel de Bordeaux which has a swimming pool. Public swimming is available at the Piscine de Picquecaillon, the Piscine Neptuna, and at the Aqua Park on the Bordeaux road. Hour-long boat trips leave Bergerac harbour at regular intervals.

Inevitably, the town has a statue to Cyrano de Bergerac, whose name also appears on many premises. It is disappointing to learn that Cyrano de Bergerac did not come from Bergerac at all; he was a Parisian who merely added a suffix to his name in order to make it more impressive.

DIVERSION TO CADOUIN

After our taste of wine, we can return to Lalinde along the D660, where we can head back to Le Bugue via Trémolat and Limeuil. However, any one of a number of side roads on the D29 east of Lalinde leads to **Cadouin**, home of a famous **abbey**. The diversion is worthwhile.

The abbey, which was founded in the twelfth century, became a place of pilgrimage when it gave a home to the Holy Shroud, a piece of embroidered linen which was said to have been the cloth that had been wrapped around Christ's head.

The shroud had been discovered by Crusaders at the church of Antioch.

Unfortunately, examination of the cloth in 1934 showed it to be a piece of eleventh century embroidered material. Pilrimages to Cadouin were discontinued.

The abbey church has a fairly austere façade and interior, in keeping with Cistercian tradition. However, very elaborate cloisters, fashioned in Flamboyant style and adorned with some very amusing sculptures, were added in the fifteenth century. There is a shroud museum in the chapter house and there is a nice timbered market hall in the square at the entrance to the church.

On my most recent visit to Cadouin, the square was full of wedding guests eagerly waiting for the appearance of the bride. When she emerged radiantly from the church, there were gasps of appreciation. As the whole village seemed to have turned out for the occasion, several able-bodied men were on hand to push the vintage wedding car which gave a succession of backfires but persistently refused to start up.

We can now return to Le Bugue, either via Trémolat or by following the D25.

Cycle Museum

Cadouin is home to the biggest **Musée du Vélocipède** in France. There are 100 exhibits and the museum traces the fascinating history of the bicycle through times of peace and war. The French passion for cycles and cycling is very evident here.

Additional Information

The Purple Périgord

Accommodation

Hôtels

Beaumont
Les Voyageurs-Tourisme
☎ 05 5322 3011
Some rooms have balconies.

Bergerac
Hôtel de Bordeaux *
☎ 05 5357 1283
40 rooms, swimming pool.

Hôtel du Commerce *
☎ 05 5327 3050
35 rooms.

Europ Hôtel *
☎ 05 5357 0654
22 rooms, swimming pool.

Hôtel la Flambée *
☎ 05 5357 5233
21 rooms, swimming pool, tennis.

Hôtel de France *
☎ 05 5357 1161
20 rooms, swimming pool.

Climat de France **
☎ 05 5357 2223

Campanile Hôtel **
☎ 05 5357 8610
46 rooms.

Hôtel Family **
☎ 05 5357 8090
8 rooms.

**** Le Moderne**
☎ 05 5357 1962
7 rooms.

Le Windsor **
☎ 05 5324 8976
50 rooms, swimming pool.

Hôtel de Provence-Tourisme
☎ 05 5357 1288
10 rooms.

Rivages Le Saint-Louis-Tourisme
☎ 05 5357 1908

Le Bugue
Domaine de la Barde *
☎ 05 5307 1654
18 rooms, swimming pool.

Royal Vézère *
☎ 05 5307 2001
53 rooms, swimming pool.

Le Cygne **
☎ 05 5307 1777
11 rooms.

Hôtel de Paris **
☎ 05 5307 2816
19 rooms.

Cadouin
Auberge de la Salvetat **
☎ 05 5363 4279
Swimmimg pool.

Issigeac
La Brucelière **
☎ 05 5358 7228

Lalinde
Le Château *
☎ 05 5361 0182
7 rooms, swimming pool, celebrated restaurant.

**** Hôtel du Périgord**
☎ 05 5361 1986

**** Jemmy Clos de la Roque**
☎ 05 5361 2327

La Résidence **
☎ 05 5361 0181
10 rooms.

Additional Information

La Forge **
☎ 05 5324 9224
15 rooms

Limeuil
Les Terrasses de Beauregard **
☎ 05 53633 3085
8 rooms, great views over the Dordogne.

Bon Accueil-Tourisme
☎ 05 5363 3097
10 rooms.

Monbazillac
Le Relais de la Diligence **
☎ 05 5358 3048
8 rooms.

Monpazier
Hôtel Edward I ***
☎ 05 5322 4400
13 rooms. Swimming pool.
Some rooms have jacuzzis.

Hôtel de Londres **
☎ 05 5322 6064. 10 rooms.

Hôtel de France *
☎ 05 5322 6601
10 rooms.

Trémolat
Le Vieux Logis ****
☎ 05 5322 8006
24 rooms, swimming pool.

Le Panoramic **
☎ 05 5322 8006
With a view of the bend in the Dordogne.

Le Périgord **
☎ 05 5322 8112

Campsites

Beaumont
Camping les Remparts **
☎ 05 5322 4086
66 emplacements, swimming pool.

Bergerac
Municipal la Pelouse **
☎ 05 5357 0667
Municipal site, 70 emplacements.

Biron
Camping le Moulinal ****
☎ 05 5340 8460
170 emplacements, swimming pool, lakeside beach, tennis, table tennis, volleyball, football, archery, horse riding, bike rental , fishing. The site is used by Keycamp.

Le Bugue
St-Avit-Loisirs ****
☎ 05 5302 6400
Holiday complex deep in the woods, just 3.7 miles (6km) from Le Bugue. Holiday homes for rent and a large number of emplacements for tents and caravans. It has indoor and outdoor pools, facilities for tennis, volleyball, archery, boules. Restaurant and evening entertainment. The site is used by Eurocamp, Keycamp and Sunsites.

La Linotte ***
☎ 05 5307 1761
88 emplacements, swimming pool.

Le Val de la Marquise ***
☎ 05 5354 7410
105 emplacements, swimming pool.

Le Rocher de la Granelle *
☎ 05 5307 2432
100 places, swimming pool, tennis.

Couze-et-St-Front
Camping des Moulins **
☎ 05 5361 1836
41 emplacements, swimming pool, tennis.

Issigeac

Camping Municipal *
☎ 05 5358 7032
21 emplacements, tennis. 1-star site.

Lalinde

Moulin de la Guillou **
☎ 05 5361 0291
100 emplacements, swimming pool,
tennis.

Camping le Parc *
☎ 05 5361 0230
27 emplacements, swimming pool.

Limeuil

Camping La Ferme des Poutiroux *
☎ 05 5363 3162
25 emplacements, swimming pool.

Monpazier

Le Moulin de David ***
☎ 05 5322 6525
100 emplacements, swimming pool,
tennis. Firework and classical music
evenings held in the summer. This is a
site recommended by the Caravan Club.

Trémolat

Camping de la Base Nautique ***
☎ 05 5322 8118
100 emplacements, swimming pool,
tennis.

Youth Hostels

The hostel at **Cadouin**
(☎ 05 5373 2878) is open all year,
except over the Christmas period.

Activity Centres

Bergerac

Boat Trips
Périgord Bagares
☎ 05 5324 5880

Bike Rental
Périgord Cycles
☎ 05 5357 0719

Le Bugue

Canoeing
Les Courrèges
☎ 05 5308 7537

Golf
Golf de la Croix de Morlemart
☎ 05 5303 2755

Monpazier

Bike Rental
J P Mouret
☎ 05 5322 6346

Trémolat

Bike Rental
Bernard Imbert
☎ 05 5322 8446

Attractions

Bergerac

Guided Tours of Town
Details from **Information Centre**
☎ 05 5357 0310

Musée du Tabac
☎ 05 5363 0413
Open: Tue to Fri 10am–12 noon, 2–
6pm; Saturday 10am–12 noon, 2–5pm;
Sun 2.30–6.30pm.

Musée du Vin
☎ 05 5363 0413
Open: Tue to Fri 10am–12 noon, 1.30–
5.30pm; Sat 10am–12 noon, 2–5pm;
Sun 2.30–6.30pm.

Biron

Château
☎ 05 535 5010
Open: every day except Mon; 10am–
7pm Jul and Aug; 10am–12.30pm, 1.30–
7pm Apr, May, Jun and Sep; 10am–
12.30pm, 1.30–5.30pm rest of year.

Continued over page...

Additional Information

Le Bugue

Aquarium du Périgord Noir
☎ 05 5307 1638
Open: every day 9am–7pm Jun, Jul and Aug; 10am–6pm Apr, May and Sep; 10am-12 noon, 2-5pm Feb, Mar, Oct, Nov.

Le Bournat village
☎ 05 5308 4199
Open: 10am–7pm May to Sep; 10am–5pm Oct and Apr.

Gouffre de Proumeyssac
☎ 05 5307 2747
1.9 miles (3km) south of le Bugue. Open: 9am–7pm Jul and Aug; 2–5pm Feb, Nov, Dec; 9.30am–12 noon, 2-5pm Mar to May and Sept to Oct.

Grotte de Bara-Bahau
☎ 05 5307 2882
1.2 miles (2km) north-west of le Bugue. Open: 8.30am–7pm Jul and Aug; 9am–12 noon, 2–7pm at other times Apr to Oct.

Terre des Oisseux
☎ 05 5307 1281
Open: 9am–8pm Jul and Aug; 9am–6pm at other times of year. In a 7-acre (2.8-hectare) park.

Cadouin

Abbey
☎ 05 5335 5040
Cloisters open every day except Tuesday. From 10am–7pm Jul and Aug; 10am-12.30pm, 1.30-5.30pm at other times of year.

Musée du Vélocipède
☎ 05 5363 4660
Open daily: 10am-7pm. One hour guided tours available.

Couze-et-St-Front

Eco Musée du Papier
☎ 05 5324 3616

Lanquais

Château
☎ 05 5361 2424
Open: every day 10am–7pm Jul and Aug; 2.30-6pm Mar, Apr, Oct, Nov, closed Tue; 10.30am-12 noon, 2.30-6.30pm May, Jun and Sep.

Monbazillac

Château
☎ 05 5361 5252
Open: 10am–7.30pm Jul, Aug; 10am–12 noon, 2–6pm Apri; 10am–12.30pm, 2–7pm May and Oct; 10am–12.30pm, 2-7.30pm Jun and Sep.

Rides in a Horse-drawn Cart
☎ 05 5358 3363

Monpazier

Guided Tour of Town
Tourist Office
☎ 05 5322 6859
11am–4pm from Apr to Oct.

Eating Out

There is no shortage of good restaurants in the Purple Périgord; many are in superb settings. A small selection follows.

Bergerac

Hôtel de Bordeaux
☎ 05 5357 1283
Has an excellent restaurant, Le Terroir, where regional dishes, including some unusual ones, are served up in a nice setting.

Le Parisien
☎ 05 535 7181
Also offers good regional cuisine and traditional dishes, but at more modest prices.

Pizzeria Gigino
☎ 05 5363 0211
In the middle of the town, offers a variety of pizza dishes, accompanied by giant salads.

Le Bugue
Le Pha
☎ 05 5308 9696
Situated by the river and adjacent to the Tourist Office, offers something different: a good selection of Asian dishes in the heartland of French cooking.

Royal Vézère
☎ 05 5307 2001
At the centre of the town and overlooking the river, has two riverside terrace restaurants, one classy and expensive, the other simpler and cheaper.

Lalinde
La Forge
☎ 05 5324 9224
Offers an alternative to the rather grand restaurants in rather grand hotels which are to be found in this area. Meals can be taken indoors, in the cosy atmosphere of a converted forge, or outside, on the terrace.

Limeuil
Les Terraces de Beauregard
☎ 05 5324 510
On the Trémolat road, has a restaurant with stunning panoramic views. There is a pretty good choice of vegetarian dishes too.

Monbazillac
La Tour des Vents
☎ 05 5358 3010
Offers panoramic views over the Bergerac vineyards to accompany *foie gras*, pigeon dishes, truffles and the like.

Monpazier
Restaurant de la Bastide
☎ 05 5322 6059
In this wonderfully-preserved walled town, has the usual offerings of *foie gras*, pigeons and truffles, but also gives you the chance to try trout with almonds.

Shopping
Many towns on our route offer opportunities for buying local products and souvenirs. Bergerac and Le Bugue both have a good range of shops and stores.

Fairs
Beaumont – second Tue of each month.
Monpazier – third Thu of each month.

Market Days
Bergerac – daily
Le Bugue – Tuesday and Saturday
Lalinde – Thu
Monpazier Saturday in season
Villeréal – Saturday. Farmers' market on Wednesday

Supermarkets
Bergerac has a Champion supermarket on the D660 and Leclerc and Intermarché supermarkets on the D933.

Syndicats d'Initiative
Cadouin   ☎ 05 5353 0609
Issigeac   ☎ 05 5358 7962
Limeuil   ☎ 05 5368 3890
Trémolat   ☎ 05 5322 8933

Tourist Information Centres
Beaumont   ☎ 05 5322 3912
Bergerac   ☎ 05 5357 031
Le Bugue   ☎ 05 5307 2048
Lalinde   ☎ 05 5361 0855
Monpazier ☎ 05 5374 3008
Villeréal ☎ 05 5336 0965

5. Sarlat Town Trail

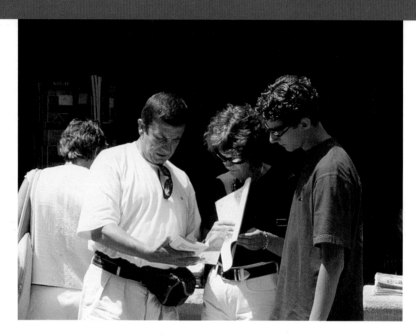

The fair face of Sarlat was formed in the medieval and Renaissance eras. Since then, the town has been subject to two major cosmetic operations: one in the nineteenth century, which badly scarred it, and one in the twentieth century, which gave it a wonderful facelift.

Let us begin at the beginning. Sarlat grew up around a Benedictine abbey, established here in the ninth century. Four centuries later, power passed from the abbots into the hands of secular 'consuls', but the fourteenth century saw the town established as an Episcopal see, with its abbey becoming a cathedral.

Sarlat grew into an important and prosperous mercantile centre and a powerful bourgeois class developed in the town. After Charles VII had granted tax concessions as reward for Sarlat's loyalty to the French crown in the Hundred Years' War, the merchants, magistrates, clerks, bishops and men of letters found they had the funds to build grand town houses, known as *hôtels*. Most of these superb buildings were erected in a golden period between 1450 and 1550.

The *hôtels* are characterised by their steeply-pitched limestone roofs, their elaborate Renaissance windows and their ornamental doorways. These

Top Tips

Sarlat

Not to be missed

- The Old Town area east of the Traverse
- Town houses, especially Maison de la Boétie, Hôtel de Maleville, Hôtel de Vassal, Hôtel de Gisson, Hôtel de Grézel
- Market day (Wednesday and Saturday)
- Cathedral of St-Sacerdos
- Lanterne des Morts

Things to do

- Take the Landmark walking tour
- Take a guided tour from the Tourist Office
- See Sarlat at night
- Visit a production in the summer Theatre Festival
- Watch street theatre
- Visit the Automobile Museum
- Visit the Wednesday or Saturday market
- Have your portrait or caricature drawn
- Have a meal in Sarlat
- Drink at a pavement café
- Have a drink at the Place de la Liberté
- Buy local crafts or a painting by a local artist
- Visit the aquarium

grand town houses are linked by narrow alleyways, small courtyards and stone staircases. It is this combination of Renaissance architecture and a medieval street pattern that gives Sarlat its unique charm.

By the nineteenth century, Sarlat had lost some of its prosperity and somewhat gone to sleep, partially because of communication problems: the town is located away from the main road and rail routes, and its own medieval street network could not accommodate increased traffic volumes. In an attempt to revive the town's fortunes, the local authority built a new road, the Rue de la République, also known as the *Traverse*, right through the heart of the town. Streets were severed and buildings were destroyed to

The Loi Malraux

André Malraux was a colourful politician, writer and soldier who had an important impact on Sarlat. Malraux served in the French army during World War II, was captured by the Germans, but escaped and fled to Roquebrune on the Riviera. In 1942, he returned to the Dordogne, where he had lived before the war, and joined the Resistance, operating under the pseudonym Colonel Berger. He was captured once again and imprisoned at Toulouse.

After the Liberation, Malraux was given the post of Minister of Propaganda, but it was during his term as Minister of Culture, between 1958 and 1968, that he made his mark on Sarlat. In 1962, he pushed through legislation that enabled large areas of towns and cities to be identified as worthy of preservation and restoration. Sarlat was chosen as a pilot scheme for putting the *Loi Malraux* into practice. More than 50 of the town's best buildings were carefully restored, with the result that Sarlat is now one of the finest and best-preserved Medieval-Renaissance towns in France.

create space for the new thoroughfare, and the town was literally slashed in two. Fortunately, almost all the great town houses survived, because they are located on the east side of the Traverse.

By the middle of the twentieth century, many of Sarlat's Medieval and Renaissance buildings and fallen into a state of neglect, but they were saved from complete dilapidation by an Act passed by the French parliament. In 1962, the Minister of Culture, André Malraux, pushed through a law that allowed a number of historic town centres to be identified as worthy of preservation and restoration. Sarlat was chosen as a pilot and restoration work began in 1964. More than fifty of the town's best buildings were renovated and 36 specially-designed street lamps

were erected in the Old Town area to give the place atmosphere. The result is one of the best-preserved Medieval-Renaissance towns in France.

Not surprisingly, Sarlat is now a magnet for visitors from all over the world and the town is highly commercialised and geared to the tourist trade. In the summer months, when its streets are teeming with tourists, car parking and even pedestrian movement can be something of a problem. Visitors should not be deterred; a visit to the town is an absolute must.

Car parking problems are at their worst on Wednesdays and Saturdays when a famous open-air market covers almost the entire town. Either arrive very early or be prepared to park in a suburb!

Travelling into Sarlat by car creates a negative first impression of the town. The road from Beynac passes the type of commercial centre which is now found on the outskirts of so many French towns: a hotchpotch of ugly, purely functional buildings, together with a collection of huge advertising signs to compete with the worst that Las Vegas has to offer. The road into the town centre is not pretty either, but does take us past an interesting **Musée de l'Automobile** with some sixty old vehicles on display.

The sloping Place de la Grande Rigaudie has a good number of marked pay-and-display parking places, but the road markings ensure that cars are very tightly packed and the car park is often full. The Place Pasteur, a little lower down the hill and behind the Police Station, offers alternative parking places.

Having parked the car, we can now set off on foot to see the Old Town. It could be argued that the best plan for seeing Sarlat is not to have a plan at all. Wandering aimlessly along the maze of alleys and stairways can bring rich rewards and unexpected delights,

Continued on page 100...

Lanterns of the dead

According to legend, Sarlat's *Lanterne des Morts* was erected to commemorate the curing of the sick by St Bernard when he came to preach in the town in 1147. It is said that people were miraculously healed when they ate bread which had been blessed by the saint.

Another story has it that the tower was used to house Sarlat's many Plague victims during the fourteenth and fifteenth centuries. A lantern at the top of the tower is said to have warned of the risk of infection, but it is very difficult to explain how a light could have been placed at the summit of this strange edifice.

Other examples of *Lanternes des Morts* are found elsewhere in the Dordogne. They are usually located in cemeteries and some have openings in their uppermost section, suggesting that lanterns could have been placed there, but Sarlat's Lantern of the Dead is well and truly enclosed, with only the merest of slits in its uppermost storey.

Most of these structures date from the twelfth or thirteenth centuries, but it is worth noting that the term *Lanterne des Morts* is a nineteenth century invention.

France: Dordogne

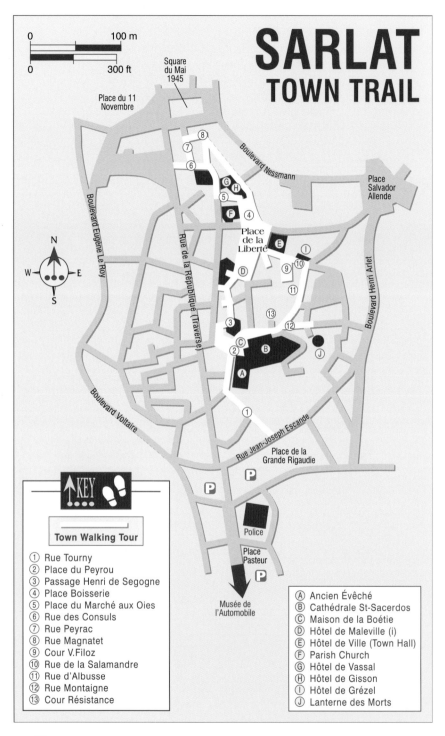

SARLAT
TOWN TRAIL

0 ————— 100 m
0 ————— 300 ft

Square du Mai 1945

Place du 11 Novembre

Boulevard Nessmann

Place Salvador Allende

Boulevard Eugène Le Roy

Boulevard Henri Arlet

Rue de la République (Traverse)

Place de la Liberté

Boulevard Voltaire

Rue Jean-Joseph Escande

Place de la Grande Rigaudie

KEY

Town Walking Tour

1 Rue Tourny
2 Place du Peyrou
3 Passage Henri de Segogne
4 Place Boisserie
5 Place du Marché aux Oies
6 Rue des Consuls
7 Rue Peyrac
8 Rue Magnatet
9 Cour V.Filoz
10 Rue de la Salamandre
11 Rue d'Albusse
12 Rue Montaigne
13 Cour Résistance

Police

Place Pasteur

Musée de l'Automobile

A Ancien Évêché
B Cathédrale St-Sacerdos
C Maison de la Boétie
D Hôtel de Maleville (i)
E Hôtel de Ville (Town Hall)
F Parish Church
G Hôtel de Vassal
H Hôtel de Gisson
I Hôtel de Grézel
J Lanterne des Morts

In the Place du Marché aux Oies

but can also result in the omission of a number of worthwhile sights. The Tourist Office offers guided walks and a number of pamphlets with helpful town maps; the Landmark tour, described in the following pages, takes in shops, restaurants, market stalls, artist quarters, the most picturesque sights and some of the town's very best buildings.

We leave the Place de la Grande Rigaudie by dropping down the Rue Tourny, where we are immediately confronted by clothes shops, souvenir outlets and restaurants. This little street gives us a flavour of what lies ahead.

Street artists

The Rue Tourny leads to the Place du Peyrou, where we find street artists at work, some of whom can produce facial likenesses in a remarkably short space of time, whilst others are able to pick out essential facial characteristics to create clever caricatures. The famous English painter David Hockney once said that he could always earn a living as a street artist if his finances ever became tight, but I wonder just how many other modern artists could match the talent of Sarlat's street artists for producing accurate portraits.

On the right, we pass the **Ancien Évêché**, a former bishop's palace, with its architectural mix of Renaissance and Gothic elements. The building is now used as a theatre and exhibition centre. Immediately after we have passed this building, we see the great bulk of the **Cathédrale St-Sacerdos**, to which we shall return later in our tour.

On the north side of the Place du Peyrou, we come face-to-face with the **Maison de la Boétie**, the first of the great town houses we will encounter on our walk. The house has a steeply pitched gable with projecting decorations, four large mullioned and transomed windows, all with highly ornate surrounds, and one fabulously decorated dormer. This fine house was built in 1525 by the father of Étienne de la Boétie, a magistrate and author, whose writings on liberty and the freedom of the individual are said to have inspired Rousseau's *Social Contract*.

An archway on the left-hand side of the building leads into the picturesque Passage Henri-de-Segogne, where there are stalls selling local goods and crafts, as well as pavement restaurants, including the nicely shaded Les Chevaliers du Tour, where English is spoken. The passage leads out onto the vast Place de la Liberté. The Tourist Office is on our left and the **Hôtel de Ville** (Town Hall) is across the square. Restaurants and pavement cafés occupy much of this large open space; the Café de la Mairie, on the forecourt of the Town Hall, is an ideal spot to have a refreshing drink, check our bearings and take in the scene.

The Office du Tourisme is housed in the **Hôtel de Maleville**, another sumptuous sixteenth century house, created by knocking together three dwellings. The combination of Italian and French Renaissance styling and the mix of tower, turret, terrace and transoms is a heady cocktail.

The Town Hall, where we have paused for refreshment, was built in the seventeenth century. Across the square, on the north-west corner of the Place de la Liberté, we can see the old Parish Church, which features a vast window which looks like the type of fenestration one would expect to find on a railway station. The building has not served as a station, but it has served at different times as an armaments store, a shopping area and a post office!

In order to continue our tour, we enter the little Place Boisserie, tucked between the church and a large flight of stone steps. This square leads us to the Place du Marché aux Oies, with an appropriate bronze statue of geese at its centre. Anyone who wishes to pose for a photograph on the statue usually has to queue and take their turn. Two more town houses, the fifteenth century **Hôtel de Vassal** and the sixteenth century **Hôtel de Gisson**, form a backdrop. The Hôtel de Gisson has two wings linked by a double staircase turret at second and third floor level. The creepers which have spread over much of the lower walls of the building add further beauty to the structure.

Just beyond the town houses, we come across a curious nave-like opening, which appears to be half man-made and half natural. The 'cave' is fronted by a fountain, but the water is not suitable for drinking. We now encounter more restaurants and a shaded niche where an artist often sets up his easel. The Rue des Consuls, on our left, has yet more restaurants. If we look ahead, we can see a half-timbered house on the continuation of this street across the Traverse. The discontinuity in the Rue des Consuls emphasises the devastating split caused when the new through road was constructed in the last century.

By walking up the Rue Peyrac and then taking a curving passage on our right, just below La Petite Italie restaurant, whose pizzas are delicious, we can leave most of the tourists behind. When we enter the Rue Magnatet, we encounter a succession of interesting houses: the first one has a terrace, the second has a jettied upper storey, the third has an ogee decoration around its doorway and the fourth is shuttered. We now walk down the flight of stone steps which we saw from the Café de la Mairie, for a wonderful view of the Place de la Liberté and St-Sacerdos Cathedral beyond.

If we now proceed to the south side of the Town Hall, we can walk up a passage containing a terrace restaurant and an art shop. The alleyway is dedicated to Véronique Filoz, painter, 1904-1977. On our left, we see an impressive studded wooden door, framed by an ogee arch, at the foot of a tower that links a half-timbered structure with a rough-stone building pierced with arrow-slits. As we have seen, linked houses are common in Sarlat. This one is the **Hôtel de Grézel**.

We are now in the Rue de la Salamandre, which leads to the Rue d'Albusse, a street whose picturesque qualities owe much to wall-mounted lamps and to shutters. This alley takes us to the side of the cathedral. By looking left up the Rue Montaigne, we can see a house with a little half-timbered tower and also the **Lanterne des Morts**, a curious cylindrical tower topped by a sugar loaf-like dome. As we drop down

France: Dordogne

Left: Place de la Liberté

Below: Maison de la Boétie

Above: A carved stone doorway, Hôtel de Grézel

Above: Caricaturist at work

the street, we can call in the Cour Résistance, a little square of artists' studios. We can then proceed to the west door of the cathedral.

Much of St-Sacerdos Cathedral dates from the rebuilding that took place in the sixteenth and seventeenth centuries, but the base of the tower is Romanesque and the bulbous belfry is eighteenth century.

We now arrive back in the Place du Peyrou which leads to the Rue Tourny and the car park, where we can begin the tricky manouevres necessary to exit from our tight parking spot.

Despite traffic and parking problems, most visitors to the Dordogne cannot resist the urge to return to Sarlat time and time again. The pull of market day, the vast choice of restaurants, the fairy-tale atmosphere of Sarlat at night and the events staged during the summer Theatre Festival all have a magnetism just too strong to resist.

Additional Information

Sarlat

Accommodation

Hotels

There is ample hotel accommodation in Sarlat at prices to suit all pockets. When making a booking, it is worth checking car parking arrangements.

Hôtel la Hoirie *
☎ 05 5359 0562
17 rooms, swimming pool.

Hôtel de la Madeleine *
☎ 05 5359 1041
39 rooms.

Relais de Moussidière *
☎ 05 5328 2874
35 rooms, swimming pool.

Hôtel la Salamandre *
☎ 05 5359 3598
35 rooms, swimming pool.

Hôtel de Selves *
☎ 05 5315 0000
40 rooms, swimming pool.

Hôtel la Charmille **
☎ 05 5359 3700
10 rooms.

Hôtel de Compostelle **
☎ 05 5359 0571
12 rooms.

Hôtel de la Mairie **
☎ 05 5359 0571
7 rooms.

Hôtel La Maison des Peyrats **
☎ 05 5359 0032
12 rooms, swimming pool.

Hôtel Marcel **
☎ 05 5359 2198
12 rooms.

Le Mas de Castel **
☎ 05 5359 0259
14 rooms, swimming pool.

Hôtel des Recollets **
☎ 05 5331 3600
18 rooms.

Hôtel Saint Albert et Montaigne **
☎ 05 5331 5555
61 rooms.

Hôtel la Verperie **
☎ 05 5359 0020
25 rooms, swimming pool.

Hôtel de la Pagézie
☎ 05 5359 3173
10 rooms, swimming pool.

Campsites

Camping le Périères ***
☎ 05 5359 0584
100 emplacements, villas for rent, swimming pool, tennis.

Moulin du Roch ***
☎ 05 5359 2027
Used by the Caravan Club. It has mobile homes, swimming pool and cycles for hire, tennis.

Le Caminel *
☎ 05 5359 3716
90 emplacements, swimming pool.

Le Rivaux **
☎ 05 5359 0441
100 emplacements.

Les Acacias **
☎ 05 5359 2930
89 emplacements, swimming pool.

Activity Centres

Horse Riding

Centre Hippique Fournier Sarlovèze
☎ 05 5359 1583

L'Étrier de Vitrac
☎ 05 5359 3431

Attractions

Aquarium
☎ 05 5359 4458
Open: 10am–7pm mid-Jun to mid-Sep; 10am–12 noon. 2.30–6pm at other times.

Bories

Cabanes de Breuil
☎ 05 5359 6444
Open: 10am–7pm Jul to Sep; 10am–12 noon, 2–7pm at other times of year.

Musée de l'Automobile
☎ 05 5331 6281
Open: 10am–10pm Jul & Aug; 10am–12 noon, 2–7pm late Mar to Jun, Sep & Oct; 10am–12 noon, 2–6pm at weekends and holidays at other times of year.

Eating Out

You will come across restaurants at every turn on the Sarlat town trail. A small selection of Sarlat restaurants follows:

Les Chevaliers du Tour
☎ 05 5331 0422
Nicely situated in the Passage de Segogne, at the heart of the Old Town. English is spoken.

Hotel de Madeleine
☎ 05 5359 1041
On the Place de la Petite Rigaudie, offers a range of regional dishes prepared by the proprietor and chef Philippe Mélot.

Restaurant Marcel
☎ 05 5359 2198
Situated on the Avenue Selves and part of the Hostellerie Marcel, offers reasonably-priced regional dishes.

Le Moulin du Roy
☎ 05 5331 1194
In the Rue Albéric Cahuet, at the heart of the Old Town, offers regional specialities at a range of prices.

La Petite Italie
☎ 05 5330 2726
On the Rue Peyrac, is a tiny restaurant, but offers diners, including vegetarians, the chance to enjoy well-cooked and reasonably-priced Italian dishes.

Le Regent
☎ 05 5359 0391
Situated in the Place de la Liberté, at the very hub of the Old Town, is a good place to people-watch, as well as eat.

Shopping

Sarlat has a wide range of shops selling souvenirs, local crafts, paintings, clothes, jewellery etc. Its open-air market is one of the finest and most extensive in France.

Market Days

Wednesday and Saturday.

Supermarkets

There are Casino, Champion and Leclerc supermarkets on the edge of town.

Tourist Information Centre

Office de Tourisme
☎ 05 5331 4545

6. The Black Périgord

First-time visitors to the Dordogne, especially those with limited time at their disposal, are likely to base their holiday in the Black Périgord, the most popular region of the Dordogne. This area contains a plethora of fairytale castles, some of the most spectacular villages in Périgord, or anywhere else for that matter, one of the finest old towns in France (see Sarlat Town Trail, Chapter 5), perhaps the most important collection of caves and prehistoric finds in the world, and some breathtaking scenery.

The Black Périgord is not just a perfect holiday destination for tourists who simply enjoy looking at interesting buildings and spending time in lovely scenery, it is also a mecca for holidaymakers who enjoy more active pursuits. This region is a paradise for canoeists, cyclists, horse-riders, hikers, photographers, artists, naturalists and even balloonists.

Opposite page: Gabare, La Roque-Gageac
Below top: Relaxing by the river,
La Roque-Gageac Below bottom:
The clinging village of Beynac

Before describing the first of our tours in this magical region, I should like to issue a reminder: visitors who spend their entire holiday in the Black Périgord will certainly have enough attractions and opportunities for outdoor pursuits to more than fill their holiday, but a skim through the previous pages of this guide will reveal how much other parts of Périgord have to offer too. Hopefully, visitors will be encouraged to explore beyond the confines of Black Périgord or be tempted to base a future holiday in the Green, White or Purple Périgord regions.

TOUR 1: THE HEART OF THE DORDOGNE

Our first tour of the Black Périgord takes in, within the space of a few miles, three of the most celebrated Dordogne villages, three stunning castles, a fine Romanesque church and irresistible opportunities for messing about on the river.

Our tour begins at Le Bugue, which was described in detail in chapter 4. We follow Sarlat signs from the town and take the D706, before turning right onto the D35 and right again on the D49.

Top Tips

Tour 1: Heart of the Dordogne
Not to be missed
- For the base town of **Le Bugue**: see previous chapter
- **St-Cyprien**: village and church
- **Beynac**: village and castle
- View from the terrace of **Beynac castle**
- **La Roque-Gageac**: village and troglodyte fort
- **Domme**: village and grotto
- Spectacular view from the terrace at Domme
- **Cénac church**, including sculptures
- **Chapelle de Caudon** (troglodyte church)
- **Castlelnaud Castle**
- **Château of Les Milandes**

Things to do
- For base town of Le Bugue: see previous chapter
- Visit the Sunday market at St-Cyprien
- Walk from St-Cyprien to Les Eyzies along the GR36
- Walk the GR64 along the Dordogne valley
- Hire a canoe or kayak at St-Vincent-de-Cosse, Vézac, Castelnaud, Cénac or Domme
- Take a boat trip from Beynac
- Travel on a barge from La Roque-Gageac
- Go ballooning from La Roque-Gageac
- Visit the caves at Domme
- Visit the Thursday market at Domme
- Have a picnic on the terrace at Domme

ST-CYPRIEN

We soon arrive at **St-Cyprien**, a village dominated by its massive church, which sits above the rippled rooftops like a great liner at anchor. The building owes its bulk to its origins as an Augustinian **abbey church**. The body of the church has been much altered over the years, but a bulky Romanesque belfry remains.

The church once attracted pilgrims, because it housed the *Sainte-Épine*, or Holy Thorn, said to have healing properties when rubbed against the clothes of sick people. It also houses the heart of Christophe de Beaumont, Archbishop of Paris. Relics not-withstanding, the building has fine seventeenth century furnishings and a wrought-iron balustrade.

The village itself, which is less pretentious than many of the show-villages of the Dordogne, is an attractive place with nice shops and cafés, including the one where I was kept waiting for half-an-hour whilst the proprietor watched television coverage of the Tour de France.

St-Cyprien's Sunday market is a wonderful affair. Car parking in the village is impossible on market day, but there is a pay-and-display car park at the foot of the village and there are kerb-side places on the little ring road. There are further shopping opportunities at the Champion supermarket in the valley below the old settlement.

The GR6 walking route runs by St-Cyprien, with a path to Les Eyzies and the valley of the Vézère to the north and a path along the Dordogne to the south.

ON TO BEYNAC

We now take the D703 along the beautiful Dordogne valley towards Beynac, passing the little golden-stone hamlet of **St-Vincent-de-Cosse** along the way. Saint Vincent is said to have been staked, flogged and finally beheaded by local druids when he tried to bring Christianity to the area. The village is nicely situated, but not easily accessible by car. Canoes are available for hire by the river.

Our next port-of-call is **Beynac**, part of the community of Beynac-et-Cazenac and one of the most stunning villages in a region teeming with show-villages.

When I was a child, my favourite book was *Five go to Smuggler's Top*. I enjoyed Enid Blyton's story-line immensely, but it was the setting for the adventure that captured my imagination: a huddled village perched on the slopes of an isolated rock. Beynac holds a special place in my affection for, in my eyes, it is Smuggler's Top made real.

The village houses, fashioned in local stone with the richest golden hue imaginable, cling, in gravity-defying manner, to a steep cliff on the banks of the Dordogne. Some have very elaborate architectural features, such as ogee decorations above their doorways. The whole village has been smartened up and prettified and its streets and alleyways have been neatly paved with setts, but the work has been carried out with such sensitivity that it is none the worse for this cosmetic operation.

Continued on page 112...

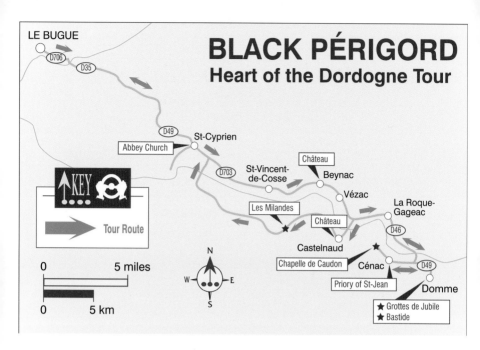

BLACK PÉRIGORD
Heart of the Dordogne Tour

LE BUGUE

D706 D35

D49 St-Cyprien

Abbey Church

KEY

Tour Route

0   5 miles

0   5 km

N
W —●●●— E
S

D703 St-Vincent-de-Cosse

Château

Beynac

Vézac

La Roque-Gageac

D46

Les Milandes ★

Château

Castelnaud

Chapelle de Caudon ★ Cénac D49

Priory of St-Jean

Domme

★ Grottes de Jubile
★ Bastide

Hut or House

During your travels through the limestone belt of the Dordogne, you may well catch an occasional glimpse of a beehive-shaped stone structure, known as a *borie*. These buildings are usually found in isolation, but there is one cluster of them at **Breuil**, near Sarlat.

Bories have cylindrical dry-stone walls and a dome-shaped roof made by a technique known as corbelling, which involves the slightly tilted stacking of layer upon layer of stones until they reach a central summit where a keystone holds the whole structure in place.

Bories are certainly very old, but their precise age is not known. They have survived to the present time, because farmers have found them useful for storage and as shelter for animals. They may have been built for these very purposes in the first place, but at least some of them could have served as living accommodation for poor peasant families.

I find it particularly interesting that beehive huts of very similar construction are also found in Ireland.

It is possible to visit the group of *bories* at Breuil.

Above: Enjoying a river trip, Beynac

Left: Shopping in Domme

Below: The road without a pavement, La Roque-Gageac

Not surprisingly, Beynac is a magnet for tourists, so parking can be something of a nightmare. There is a fair-sized pay-and-display car park by the river, and I would advise visitors to circle round this parking lot a few times and exercise patience. Spaces do appear from time to time! There is a good little Information Centre by the car park and there are some very nice hotels and cafés on the quayside. A wander up the cliff-side alleyways is a must, both to inspect the picturesque cottages and to catch the fabulous view over the river. The river itself is incredibly busy with canoes and pleasure boats. Canoes and kayaks can be hired at Port d'Enveaux, at St-Vincent-de-Cosse, and 50 minute boat trips, with commentary in English, German, Dutch and French, leave Beynac quayside at half-hourly intervals in high season.

There is an equestrian centre at Le Castanet, where the proprietors speak English, Dutch and German, and there is a municipal tennis court. A 3-star campsite, Le Cape-yrou, has 100 emplacements.

Vézac, just down river from Beynac, has two canoe hire centres, two campsites and a beach.

LA ROQUE-GAGEAC

As if the theatrical setting of Beynac were not drama enough, we next come to **La Roque-Gageac**, a village

Beynac's castle

The feudal origins of Beynac are very evident. The clinging village is dominated by the massive cliff-top château, ancestral seat of one of the four baronies of Périgord. The castle can be reached by a steep footpath or by car, via a 2-mile (3km) road that winds its way up the hill; on the way up, we catch sight of a conical stone hut in a field, known as a *borie*. These are not uncommon in this part of the Dordogne. Parking at the entrance to the castle is pay-and-display.

The golden-stone texture of the great fortress is in perfect harmony with the village at its foot and the great cliff on which it stands. The castle has a colourful history too: it was captured by Richard the Lionheart, used as a headquarters by the ruthless Mercadier, ravaged by Simon de Montfort and then rebuilt by the lords of Beynac, and used in the latter part of the Hundred Years' War as a French stronghold. The English stronghold was at Castelnaud, across the river, and the two castles seem to glare across the Dordogne at each other even now!

A visit to the castle is not to be missed. The guide opens the door with a huge key and leads visitors to the Great Hall of State, with its barrel roof, and the oratory, with its impressive frescoes. The view from the terrace, a sheer 450ft (140m) above the Dordogne, is utterly breath-taking.

which is even more daring than Beynac in its determination to cling on to an almost vertical cliff-side, so much so, in fact, that some houses actually perished in a cliff fall in 1956. We pass La Roque-Gageac's castle, a picturesque nineteenth century copy of a fifteenth century château, on our way into this most photographed of French villages.

There is ample parking in the large riverside car park at the far end of the village, but it is not easy to be a pedestrian in La Roque-Gageac. The wonderfully picturesque terrace of quayside houses, with their distinctive steeply-pitched roofs, fronts right onto the busy D703 and there is no pavement. Following a spell of traffic-dodging and a relaxing drink at a quayside café, you will also want to climb one of the steep alleyways to the cliff-side dwellings and the troglodyte fort. After struggling up the cliff, you will almost certainly be ready for another cool drink at a pavement café.

If you would like to stay in this highly picturesque and hugely popular (therefore crowded) village, there are no fewer than four campsites and three 2-star hotels.

We leave La Roque-Gageac by the D703 and then take the D46 and D49 to **Domme**, yet another stunning village, but one that sits at the summit of a sheer cliff, rather than on its slopes.

DOMME

Domme is a *bastide* town, founded in 1281 by Philip the Bold. It has all the usual ingredients found in *bastides*: town walls, fortified gateways (Porte de la Combe, Porte del Bos and Porte

River activities

La Roque-Gageac is a former inland port for the export of wine and timber, but its river is still a hive of activity, attracting swarms of holidaymakers eager to paddle along one of the most beautiful stretches of the Dordogne. It is possible to hire a one-person kayak, canoes for two, three or four people, or to take a voyage on an eight or ten-passenger canoe piloted by a guide. Alternatively, visitors can glide down the river as passengers on a traditional boat (*gabare*). It is even possible to take to the air in a hot-air balloon (contact Montgolfière du Périgord).

des Tours, the last of which acted as a prison for the Knights Templars), a covered market hall and streets laid out in a grid pattern. But Domme has more charm than the strictly rectangular bastides of the Purple Périgord, because the town is made irregular, despite its rectilinear street pattern, by the uneven terrain on which it is built and because the fortification on one side of the town is not man-made, but rather the cliff-side itself.

The houses of Domme are self-consciously pretty. Some have scroll-style dormers, many have balconies and most are festooned with geraniums. Cars have to be left at the foot of the village, so it is possible to wander the streets in safety whilst hunting for souvenirs. The wide choice of gifts includes

An Indomitable (or in-Domme-itable) Soldier

Domme remained staunchly Catholic during the Wars of Religion. The Protestant captain Geoffroi de Vivans had already made two abortive attempts to capture the town when he hit upon a new plan of attack.

As we have seen, Domme is defended by gates and walls on three sides, but protected on the fourth side by a sheer cliff, known as the *Barre*. During one night in 1588, Vivans assembled the bulk of his troops outside the walls of the town and told them to remain quiet. He then went off with thirty or so men to climb the *Barre* under cover of darkness. After reaching the summit, the group entered the town and started banging, clattering and shouting, in order to create cacophonous mayhem. During the confusion, Vivans' men were able to open the town gates to let in the bulk of the forces who then duly captured the town.

Vivans held Domme for four years, during which time he destroyed Catholic places of worship, but then added insult to injury by selling the settlement back to the Catholics.

It is also claimed that Vivans captured nearby Sarlat during the town's carnival celebrations by disguising his men as harlequins!

Old gate to Town

excellent toys for children and trinkets for young visitors. The town holds a Thursday market, when parking really is impossible.

The Market Hall makes an unusual entrance to the **Grottes de Jubile**, a network of underground caves which have often served as refuges for the townspeople in times of war. The grottoes, with their good, illuminated stalactites and stalagmites, make a worthwhile visit.

The church at Cénac

The real attraction of Domme, in my eyes, is the marvellous view of the Dordogne countryside from the esplanade at the summit of the cliff on which the town is built. The panorama provides an interesting contrast with the patchwork-quilt appearance of the English countryside, where field divisions pick out and exaggerate the natural contours. There are far fewer hedgerows to provide visual relief in France than there are in England. At ground level, the French countryside is seen to stretch uninterruptedly to far horizons, but from this bird's-eye-view the landscape is revealed as a rich collage of geometric shapes. Seen in miniature from Domme's belvedere, the fields of Périgord look like the floor of a carpet warehouse where various mats and rugs have been laid out for inspection.

CÉNAC

From Domme, we take the D49 down to **Cénac**, where there are camp-sites, canoe hire centres, the GR64 walking route and a beach. Cénac is really Domme-by-the-River. The village also has an architectural gem: the Priory of **St-Julien**, located just beyond the settlement. The church, which was built in the twelfth century, but partially destroyed by Geoffroi de Vivans in the Wars of Religion, was restored in the nineteenth century. The exterior is very beautiful, despite the clear contrast between old and newer stonework, but the interior is even more striking, as it contains a dazzling array of sculptures depicting animals and humans engaged in a range of activities, including a pig devouring human heads, Daniel in the lions' den, naked dancers and a lustful snake between two naked ladies.

Just down the road, there is another remarkable, but very different church: the little troglodyte **Chapelle de Caudon**, built by persecuted Catholics at the time when Domme was under Protestant occupation.

CASTELNAUD

If we now back-track to the D703 and then turn left over the Dordogne, we come to the riverside settlement of **Castelnaud**, where a magnificent fortress stands in thick woods, high above the village. This was an English stronghold in the Hundred Years' War and the great rival to Beynac Château across the river. The castle houses a museum devoted to warfare

Rainbow Warrior

Josephine Baker was born in St Louis, Missouri in 1906. It is said that her family was so poor that her sleeping arrangements took the form of a box that she shared with a dog. She began her professional career as a chorus girl in America, but made her name in Paris by dancing the Black Bottom whilst wearing nothing but a string of bananas. She became the toast of the Folies Bergères and the highest paid entertainer in Europe.

The performer adopted French citizenship in 1937 and worked for the Resistance during the war, helping a number of people to escape Nazi persecution. She was awarded the *Croix de Guerre* for her efforts.

The dancer bought Les Milandes, spent large sums on its restoration and even opened a restaurant and, later, a casino there. But Josephine Baker now used her energy, which had been harnessed to such good effect in the music halls and in the war effort, in the cause of children. She adopted a number of multi-racial orphaned children, known as the 'Rainbow Tribe', and housed them and cared for them at Les Milandes.

Unfortunately, the costs of restoring and maintaining the castle, along with the investment in raising her adopted family, proved too great, and she was forced to sell the château.

Château of les Milandes, the former home of Josephine Baker

Hat Tricks

Roofs are one of the delights of Périgord architecture, and nowhere more so than in the town of Domme.

Insertions always add interest to roofscapes. Dormers are commonly found on Dordogne houses, and those on the grander houses are sometimes adorned with elaborate stone surrounds. Scroll-shaped settings are characteristically found on Domme's dormers. The triangular openings, known as *outeaux*, which puncture some other roofs, are designed to ventilate the upper storeys.

A variety of roofing material is to found in Périgord. Stone flags (*lauzes*) are commonly used on roofs in the limestone regions, but flat clay tiles or even curved Roman tiles are used in other areas.

Dordogne roofs are usually steeply-pitched, but the angle of the roof is often shallower near its base, where the roof is kicked out over the walls to protect them from rain. This arrangement creates a rather appealing wide-brimmed hat look to some buildings. Materials and stacking arrangements may also change in the lower reaches of the roof where curved tiles are often preferred to flat ones.

There is a particularly fine example of mixed roofing materials on a house near the car park at the entrance to Domme.

in the Middle Ages. The château is open during the day, and late night tours, which include a specially created spectacle, can be made on any weekday evening from early July to late August.

There are two 3-star campsites at Castelnaud, a kayak club and an equestrian centre trading as La Vallée des Châteaux.

BACK TO LE BUGUE

We can now carry on along the south bank of the river and then follow signposts up a hill to **Les Milan-** **des**. The château, with its beautiful French gardens, was once the home of the entertainer Josephine Baker and her adopted family of multi-racial children. The building, which is open every day, contains period furniture, some splendid stained glass, a Josephine Baker Museum and a Museum of Falconry. Regular falconry displays are held.

We can now meander along the quiet roads on the south bank of the Dordogne, until we reach a bridge which takes us back across the river to the D703 for St-Cyprien and Le Bugue, where we can sit with a glass of wine and reflect on a journey to remember.

TOUR 2: THE CRADLE OF MANKIND

Tableau in the Préhisto Parc, Tursac

INTRODUCTION

Our first tour from Sarlat, and our second venture into the Black Périgord, takes us to Les Eyzies, known as the Capital of Prehistory, and along the Vézère Valley, often dubbed the Cradle of Mankind.

The limestone cliffs of this region are honeycombed with prehistoric cave shelters and grottoes that have yielded thousands of clues about the everyday life of prehistoric man, as well as graphic and colourful evidence of his surprising artistic talent. The shelters and their rock paintings are so amazing and so improbably numerous that one is tempted to doubt their authenticity. But who am I to cast doubt? So many experts can't be wrong. Can they?

The caves are scattered liberally in the cliffs and woods around Les Eyzies. As some are quite difficult to locate and as it would be impossible to find the time to visit all of them, this chapter includes easy-to-follow directions from the village of Les Eyzies to a selection of prehistoric sites and grottoes. An early start is needed on a cave-visiting day as some of the show caves require tickets to be bought at the beginning of morning or afternoon sessions.

The Cradle of Mankind Tour is not simply concerned with pre-history. Our trip takes us through some beautiful countryside and includes visits to some of the most attractive châteaux in Périgord and opportunities to enjoy some exquisite villages.

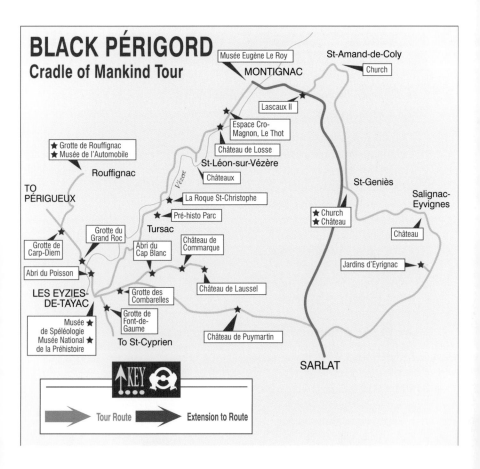

BLACK PÉRIGORD
Cradle of Mankind Tour

Musée Eugène Le Roy

MONTIGNAC

St-Amand-de-Coly

Church

Lascaux II

Espace Cro-Magnon, Le Thot

★ Grotte de Rouffignac
★ Musée de l'Automobile

Rouffignac

Château de Losse

St-Léon-sur-Vézère

Châteaux

St-Geniès

Salignac-Eyvignes

TO PÉRIGUEUX

La Roque St-Christophe

Pré-histo Parc

★ Church
★ Château

Château

Grotte du Grand Roc

Tursac

Grotte de Carp-Diem

Abri du Cap Blanc

Château de Commarque

Jardins d'Eyrignac

Abri du Poisson

LES EYZIES-DE-TAYAC

Grotte des Combarelles

Château de Laussel

Musée ★ de Spéléologie
Musée National ★ de la Préhistoire

Grotte de Font-de-Gaume

To St-Cyprien

Château de Puymartin

SARLAT

KEY

Tour Route   Extension to Route

THE TOUR:
SARLAT
TO LES EYZIES

Shortly after leaving the centre of Sarlat, we take a left fork on the D47 for Les Eyzies. The road twists and turns along a pretty valley formed by a river known as the Petite Beune. We need to keep a careful watch for the direction sign to the **Château de Puymartin**, which stands high in the woods to our right. (see box on Château de Puymartin on page 121).

As we approach Les Eyzies-de-Tayac, the landscape is increasingly dominated, both on our flanks and straight ahead, by great limestone cliffs, many of which are pock-marked with caves and shelters: we are now entering the area known as the Cradle of Mankind. Since the first unearthing of bones and carved flints in a shelter at Madeleine in 1862, the area around Les Eyzies has seen the discovery of a large number of cave shelters and yielded a plethora of prehistoric remains,

Top Tips

Tour 2: Cradle of Mankind

Not to be missed

- Château de Puymartin
- **National Museum of Prehistory**, Les Eyzies
- **Pré-histo Parc**, Tursac
- La Roque-St-Christophe
- Village of **St-Léon-sur-Vézère**
- Château de Losse
- **Lascaux II** and the **Museum of Prehistory** Le Thot
- **Church** at **St-Amand-de-Coly**
- Village of **St-Geniès**
- **Château** of **Salignac-Eyvignes**
- The **gardens of Eyrignac**

At least some of the following caves are recommended:

- Abri du Cap Blanc
- Abri du Poisson
- Grotte des Combarelles
- Grotte de Font-de-Gaume
- Grotte du Grand Roc
- Grotte de Rouffignac

Things to do

- Take a detour to the Château de Laussel along the D48
- Buy local produce, fossils or souvenirs in Les Eyzies
- Watch the world go by from a café in Les Eyzies
- Buy Bergerac wine from a road-side stall near Les Eyzies
- Photograph geese near Tursac
- Have a picnic in the Pré-histo Parc
- Pause for refreshment (picnic, drink or meal) at St-Léon-sur-Vézère
- Admire the view from the terrace of the Château de Losse
- Take a detour to St-Geniès to admire the frescoes
- Inspect perfect topiary at the gardens of Eyrignac
- Canoe along the Vézère from Les Eyzies, St-Léon-sur-Vézère or Montignac
- Go horse riding from Tamniès or Tursac

Château de Puymartin

Puymartin is one of my favourite Dordogne castles. The château, which has been the home of the de Marzac family for 500 years, was built by the St Clar family in the fifteenth and sixteenth centuries. Although it was much restored in the nineteenth century, the castle remains an archetypal Dordogne residence in combining the comfort and delicate beauty of a Renaissance-style château with defensive characteristics, such as keeps, turrets, pepperot towers and battlements. The furniture, from various pre-Revolutionary periods, the Aubusson tapestries, which trace the history of the Trojan War, and the wall paintings, with their mythological themes, all add elegance to the castle, but Puymartin manages to have a nice homely feel about it.

including skeletons, tools, domestic utensils, weapons, jewellery, ornaments and cave paintings. At the entrance to Les Eyzies, we are confronted by a bewildering array of advertisements and signposts for caves. If we were to follow all of them we would condemn ourselves to a lengthy subterranean holiday and we would also have some difficulty in locating some of the sites. Some careful planning and navigation is necessary if we are to map out a sensible 'prehistory route'. Let us begin our explorations by making a short detour from the D47 along the D48.

A right turn along the D48 takes us to the **Abri du Cap-Blanc**. This is the shelter where a frieze of rock sculptures was found in 1909. The carvings, which clearly depict horses and bison-like creatures, stand out in relief from the walls of the cave and have an uncanny three-dimensional appearance.

If we carry on along the D48, we come to the **Château de Commarque**, a ruined castle set splendidly on the banks of the Beune, and then the little, much restored **Château de Laussel**, set on a high cliff above the river. It always strikes me that this little diversion along the D48 would have appealed greatly to the romantic spirit of Victorian travellers. We now retrace our route back to the D47.

Just before entering the village of Les Eyzies, we encounter signposts for the **Grotte des Combarelles**. This cave, discovered in 1901, is essentially a long tunnel whose walls are decorated with hundreds of drawings of animals from the Magdelanian period (15,000 to 10,000 BC). Some of the drawings are open to various interpretations and others only take on representational qualities when cleverly illuminated, but there can be no doubt that this cave contains rich evidence of man's early artistic talent.

LES EYZIES-DE-TAYAC

The village of **Les Eyzies** is dominated by a statue of **Cro-Magnon Man** that peers down on the settlement from a limestone ridge. The large sculpture,

Fancy Pigeonniers for pigeon fanciers

Pigeonniers (or dovecotes) are a fairly common sight in Périgord. Always raised above ground level in order to keep out damp and pests, they either take the form of towers attached to dwellings or free-standing structures supported on arches or columns. This Tursac pigeonnier is a fine example of a column-mounted, free-standing dovecote.

In pre-Revolutionary France, the keeping of pigeons was usually reserved for the more powerful landowners, but this was not the case in Périgord, where anyone could keep pigeons in return for a fee. Pigeons were highly valued: they were a good source of food, particularly when other sources of meat were scarce; their droppings were used as fertilizer, as a cure for goitre and even as a means of adding aroma to bread. In fact, the village bread oven was often located in the ground floor of a *pigeonnier*!

Cro-Magnon man at Les Eyzies

carved by Paul Dardé in 1930, represents the human form indicated by the 35,000 year-old skeletons that were discovered in the Cro-Magnon cave in 1868 during the construction of a new railway line.

Les Eyzies is not a particularly pretty village, but it is unashamedly a tourist centre. Parking is not easy at times, although there is some on-street meter parking, and pedestrians are hampered by the wooden cut-outs of geese outside shops selling *foie gras*, as well as the large barrels which indicate outlets for wine. There are shops selling fossils, with ammonites galore, and trinket shops selling little statues of Cro-Magnon man (not a pretty sight!). Delicious local fruit and vegetables are on sale, as well as some of the nicest biscuits that you will ever taste.

As Les Eyzies stands at a cross-roads, the flow of traffic is unrelenting, but it is noticeable that some tourists show suicidal tendencies by dodging in and out of the cars in an attempt to find a suitable spot from which to point their cameras up at Cro-Magnon man and that cyclists are willing to brave the traffic as they converge on the village from all directions. Sitting at a pavement café here is like taking a seat in the Tower of Babel, with languages from all over the world emanating from the passing stream of tourists. I have to confess that I rather like all this activity, despite the blatant commercialism.

Having been suitably educated about speleology and prehistory, we can now set off to explore some of the caves in the immediate vicinity of Les Eyzies.

Les Eyzies has two important museums. **The Musée National de Préhistoire**, housed in a fortress in the cliff that overhangs the village, contains a large collection of prehistoric finds, including bones, primitive utensils, ornaments and weapons, castings of wall paintings and stone sculptures. **The Musée de la Spéléologie**, along the Périgueux road, contains caving equipment and geological information relating to caves and subterranean formations.

If we drop down the D48 road towards St-Cyprien for a short distance, we come to the **Grotte de Font-de-Gaume**, a cave with many wall paintings, including some highly colourful ones. The paintings of animals are not only remarkably life-like, they also strongly suggest movement. Many different animal species are depicted and some paintings are superimposed on older pictures. The 45-minute guided tours must be booked in advance.

DETOUR TO THE NORTH-WEST

A detour from Les Eyzies along the D47 takes us firstly to the **Abri du Poisson**, a cave shelter with a 3ft (1m) long, 20,000 year old carving of a fish. The picture is so accurate and carefully detailed that one is left wondering just how much tinkering and highlighting was undertaken by the restorers. But I must not be sceptical: this is a significant

find. Tickets for the 45-minute guided tour must be booked at the Grotte de Font-de-Gaume.

We next come to the **Grotte du Grand Roc**, a cave noted for its splendid location high above the Vézère and its collection of stalagmites and stalactites. Forty-five-minute guided tours are available. Signs now lead us to the **Grotte de Carp-Diem**, another treasure house of stalagmites and stalactites which is open daily, and the **Grotte de Rouffignac**, where visitors are carried by train to see wall engravings of animals, including herds of mammoths in combat. **Rouffignac** also has a **Musée de l'Automobile**, housed in the Château de Fleurac. The château was built in the nineteenth century.

BACK TO OUR TOUR – ON TO MONTIGNAC

If we now return to Les Eyzies, we can continue our tour along the D706 to Montignac. Two roadside attractions will cause us to stop: a wine stall selling some excellent bottles of Bergerac wine, and a farmyard teeming with photogenic flocks of geese, blissfully unaware of the fate that awaits them. We also pass some beautiful honey-coloured farmsteads and a fine **pigeonnier**, standing alone in a field on our left.

At Tursac, we arrive at the **Pré-histo Parc**, one of Périgord's most popular attractions. A forest framed by limestone cliffs has been laid out with a discovery trail, which takes us along a path past tableaux depicting scenes from the daily lives of Cro-Magnon and Neanderthal people, with natural niches in the cliffs being cleverly utilised to represent prehistoric shelters. It is disappointing to find that the explanatory plaques on the tableaux are exclusively in French, although guidebooks in English are on sale. Some of the tableaux are accompanied by impressive sound effects, but as these are only switched on periodically, synchronisation is sometimes lacking. One might easily be looking at a quiet domestic scene whilst hearing the noise of a chase from a hunting scene a few yards down the path!

Although my eight year old daughter struggled somewhat with the rather quaint and quasi-scientific language in the little English guidebook, she voted the Pré-histo Parc a hit, describing the trail as "much better at bringing prehistory to life than a collection of bones". At the end of the trail, there is a shop, a good snack bar and a nice picnic area in a shaded corner of the woods.

Our next stop along the D706 is at **La Roque-St-Christophe**, a sheer, half-mile (1km) long wall of limestone alongside a beautiful stretch of the Vézère. The cliff is pierced by rows of caves on a number of different levels, linked by staircases carved from the rock. Some of the caves date from the Palaeolithic era, but the cliff was also used as a fort during the Hundred Years' War. There are 45 minute guided tours in July and August.

The D706 then passes close by **St-Léon-sur-Vézère**. We have a good many reasons to pause here. The settlement has one castle in the square and another by the river; there is a lovely church and the village is full of golden stone houses festooned with creepers and geraniums. We can picnic by the river or have a refreshing drink at a pavement café in front of the *tabac* or, more grandly, enjoy a meal at Le Petit Léon restaurant. Canoes can be hired here and St-Léon has a superbly equipped campsite with the apt name of Le Paradis, as well as hotel accommodation at the Relais de St-Léon.

After returning to the D706 and driving along for a few miles, we catch site of a perfectly proportioned castle in the fields on our right. This is the fourteenth to sixteenth century **Château de Losse** on the banks of the Vézère. Its rooms contain furniture from various periods and some noted seventeenth century tapestries. The view from the terrace is sublime.

On our approach to **Montignac**, we pass the **Espace Cro-Magnon, Le Thot**. As this exhibition space is partly devoted to an account of the development of cave painting, it is an ideal prelude to a visit to the **Lascaux Caves** located at the other side of town. It is possible to buy a ticket for the museum alone or a joint ticket for the museum and the Lascaux caves. During July and August, tickets can only be purchased from the information points in Montignac. Be warned: early booking is essential and you may have to wait some time for your allocated visiting slot.

Montignac is a nice old town, memorable for its riverside houses, many of which have balconies supported on

Continued on page 128...

125

Above & right: Wine stall near Les Eyzies

Below: Geese near Tursac

One boy and his dog

One day in 1940, a boy called Ravidat was out walking with three friends when his dog, named Robot, disappeared down a hole. Ravidat used a knife to widen the entrance to the hole and went in pursuit of his pet and found himself in a large cave. The boys returned with torches to explore the caverns further and, to their great surprise, discovered paintings on the walls.

When the boys' schoolteacher heard of their discovery, he contacted Abbé Breuil, a leading authority on prehistory. Investigation revealed that the caves contain some 1,500 prehistoric pictures, some carved, others painted. Recognising the importance of the discovery, the Abbé dubbed the Lascaux caves the 'Sistine Chapel of Périgord'.

Just as chance had led to the discovery of these works of art, so good fortune had played a major role in their survival. An impermeable layer of rock above the roof of the cave had helped to keep out water, a calcite deposit had formed a protective layer on their surface, and a rock-fall had sealed the cave entrance and kept out both intruders and contaminated air.

The caverns were opened as show-caves in 1948, but more damage was done in the fifteen years during which the caves were open to the public than in the previous 15,000 years. To prevent further damage from the carbon dioxide expired by visitors, the caves were closed in 1963 and replaced ten years later by replica caves.

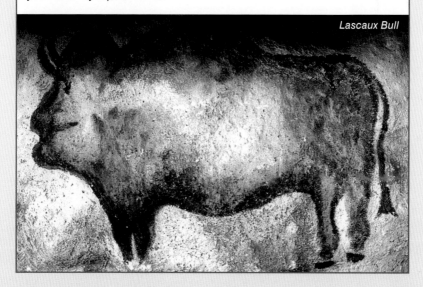

Lascaux Bull

The reindeer age

Although experts insist that Neanderthal man is a remote cousin of modern man, rather than a direct ancestor, the Neanderthal people depicted in the tableaux at the Pré-histo Parc bear a reasonable resemblance to present-day humans. However, most of the animals depicted in these tableaux are markedly dissimilar to species currently found in southern France.

The Upper Palaeolithic period is sometimes dubbed the Reindeer Age, because it is assumed that reindeer formed the staple diet of Neanderthal man. This is reflected in a number of the Pré-histo depictions, but animals in other tableaux include a now extinct stag-like creature called a megaceros, a woolly rhinoceros, a mammoth, a cave lynx, cave lions and cave hyenas.

When the climate warmed up, some 10,000 years ago, the reindeer, mammoths and some other creatures moved north to colder regions and some human hunters migrated with them. Other humans stayed put and sought new resources, which all goes to prove just how resourceful and adaptable we are as a species.

rather precarious stilts. There is a ruined castle, a château-like hotel, the Hôtel de Bouilhac, on the hill above the town, and the **Musée Eugène le Roy,** adjacent to the *syndicat d'initiative*, that contains a display of local arts and crafts and a reconstruction of the study where le Roy wrote his history of the Peasants' Revolt.

We can now return to Sarlat along the D704, but we may be tempted by a detour along the D64. This road first leads us to **St-Amand-de-Coly**, a village with a large fortified church which has a huge niche in its massive tower. The church is so obviously a defensive structure that some old documents actually refer

Lascaux show caves

A winding road from Montignac climbs up to the Lascaux show caves (remember: tickets can only be purchased in the town). The caves containing the Lascaux cave paintings were discovered in 1940 and opened to the public in 1948, but they closed in 1963 when it became obvious that the carbon dioxide breathed out by more than one million visitors was damaging the paintings. Ten years later, an imaginative scheme was hatched to create an exact replica of the caves and their works of art. These caves, known as **Lascaux II**, were opened to the public in 1983.

The tour of Lascaux II begins in a small underground interpretation centre and exhibition space and then moves on to the Hall of Bulls, with its depictions of a herd of black bulls, including one 16ft (5m) painting of a bull. Other animals, especially horses, are depicted here and in the adjacent cave. The Well Gallery contains the famous painting of a wounded bison, together with a falling man. The fact that Lascaux II is a copy does not diminish the impact of the visit. Like everyone else I have met who has visited the caves, I am astonished and overwhelmed by this amazing display of prehistoric art. So many questions are posed. How could these paintings survive so well across the centuries? How could so-called primitive people show such skill? Why were the paintings created? Was the cave a home or a shrine?

to it as a 'fort'. The nice village of **St Geniès** comes next. Here we find a ruined castle, another fortified church and the **Chapelle du Cheylard**, on a mound behind the Post Office. The chapel has some exceptional frescoes. The D64 joins the D60 which takes us to the **Château de Salignac-Eyvignes**, which has the appearance of a medieval fortress, but a Renaissance interior. The castle is closed on Tuesdays, but guided tours are available on other days in high season. The D61 takes us to the **Jardins d'Eyrignac**, eighteenth century formal gardens with very impressive examples of topiary art. The gardens are open every day.

We can now follow the D61 and then the D47 to Sarlat.

TOUR 3: THE PILGRIMAGE

Fénelon's Tower, Carennac

INTRODUCTION

Visits to some outstanding villages have been a feature of all our tours around the four tourist regions of Périgord, but visits to two of the most memorable villages have been saved for our final trip. Carennac, a settlement founded around a deanery in the tenth century, is my own favourite Dordogne village. Rocamadour, the ultimate destination on our final tour, is the most spectacular of all the Dordogne's spectacular villages, a famous pilrimage centre and one of

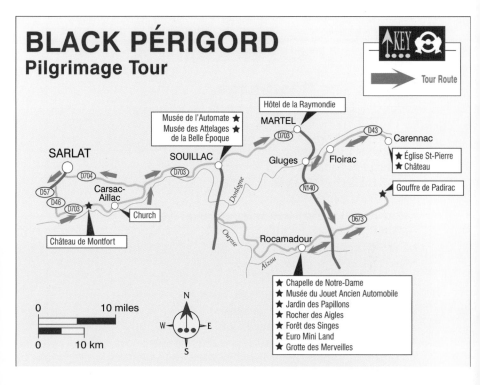

BLACK PÉRIGORD
Pilgrimage Tour

KEY

→ Tour Route

Musée de l'Automate ★
Musée des Attelages ★
de la Belle Époque

Hôtel de la Raymondie
MARTEL
D703

D43
Carennac

SARLAT

SOUILLAC
D703

Gluges
Floirac

★ Église St-Pierre
★ Château

D704

D57
D46
D703

Carsac-
Aillac

N140

Gouffre de Padirac

Church

Dordogne

D673

Château de Montfort

Ouysse

Rocamadour

Aizou

0   10 miles

0   10 km

N
W   E
S

★ Chapelle de Notre-Dame
★ Musée du Jouet Ancien Automobile
★ Jardin des Papillons
★ Rocher des Aigles
★ Forêt des Singes
★ Euro Mini Land
★ Grotte des Merveilles

the most visited places in France.

Our tour also takes us along one of the most beautiful stretches of the Dordogne river and through some of the thick woods that have given rise to the Black Périgord's name. This final visit includes yet more castles and two market towns, one bustling and full of holidaymakers, the other a fine medieval survival.

THE TOUR BEGINS – SARLAT TO SOUILLAC

We begin our journey in the Black Périgord by taking a circuitous route from Sarlat to Souillac. We follow the D57 towards Beynac but, shortly after passing the junction with the D704, we turn left along the D46 towards **Montfort**. As we approach the Dordogne river, we take another left turn along the D703 for a splendid riverside route to Souillac.

The scenery is idyllic, with golden rocks on our left and the peaceful river on our right. Tranquillity is replaced quite suddenly by drama as we catch our first sight of a fairytale castle – Château de Montfort – perched on a sheer cliff above a huddled village of golden stone.

The castle was named, with more than a touch of irony, after Simon de Montfort who captured and destroyed it in 1214. It was subsequently acquired and rebuilt by the Turenne family, only to be captured by the English in

Top Tips

Tour 3: The Pilgrimage

Not to be missed

- **Cingle de Montfort**
- **Church at Carsac-Aillac**
- **Château de Fénelon**
- **Abbey church at Souillac**
- **St Martin's Belfry** at Souillac
- **Mechanical toy and horse-drawn carriage museums** at Souillac
- **Martel**: the Old Town
- The view of **Gluges village**
- **Carennac**: village, portal, cloisters
- **Gouffre de Padirac**
- **Rocamadour**: village, sacred sites, views
- **Museum of Sacred Art**, Rocamadour
- **Euro Mini Land**, near Rocamadour
- **Forêt des Singes** (Monkeyland) near Rocamadour
- **Rocher des Aigles** (birds of prey) near Rocamadour
- **Butterfly park**, near Rocamadour

Things to do

- Play golf or swim or play tennis at Vitrac
- Hire a canoe at Vitrac or Carsac
- Enjoy the panorama at the Cingle de Montfort
- Buy truffles on the way to Souillac
- Shop in Souillac
- Take a petit train ride in Souillac
- Stop at a café in Souillac
- Visit the market at Souillac
- Picnic outside the Old Town at Martel
- Visit the market at Martel
- Fish in the Dordogne at Carennac
- Take a riverside walk at Carennac
- Descend halfway to hell at Padirac
- Walk the pilgrims way up the steps at Rocamadour (or take the lift)
- Take a petit train ride in Rocamadour
- Photograph Rocamadour when it is floodlit
- Buy truffles in Rocamadour
- Watch birds of prey from the Rocher des Aigles

the Hundred Years' War, before being recovered by the Turennes and turned into a Huguenot stronghold during the Wars of Religion. The present, highly photogenic appearance of the castle owes much to a nineteenth century restoration.

After passing Montfort village, the road climbs a ridge above a loop (*cingle*) in the Dordogne. At the summit, there is a pull-in where we can enjoy a fine panorama. The view would be memorable without the backdrop of the château on its great ridge of golden stone, but the mix of natural and man-made elements makes this an unforgettable scene. Man and nature have combined in the most spectacular fashion.

The road now takes us down to the little hamlet of **Carsac-Aillac**, where we can pull into a parking area on our left and inspect a less dramatic, but no less exquisite set-piece. A simple church of honey-coloured stone stands deep in the valley next to a balustraded house. The church has a pointed bell-tower and a beautiful roof of stone *lauzes*. The interior has richly decorated bosses and capitals and, surprisingly, some twentieth century stained glass.

After Carsac, we join the D704 very briefly, before following the D703 once again for Souillac. The road now passes through thickly-wooded countryside, reminding us that the Black Périgord is as well-wooded today as England was in pre-Industrial Revolution times. On our right, we catch sight of the **Château de Fénelon**, birthplace of Fénelon, the author of *Les Aventures de Télémarque*. We shall hear more of Fénelon when we arrive at Carennac, but we can view his bedroom by

taking a trip around the castle, which is heavily fortified and has buildings dating from the fifteenth to the seventeenth century.

SOUILLAC

As we approach **Souillac**, there is a marked change of texture. Golden stone, which has so beautifully clothed all the villages along the Dordogne from Limeuil to Carsac-Aillac, gives way to white limestone. The scene also becomes much busier, with a railway on our left and much commercial activity, some of it centred on the sale of truffles. We soon find ourselves in the outskirts of Souillac.

As Souillac stands at a busy crossroads and as the streets of its old town are narrow, finding a parking place can be difficult, but it is worth following the signs to a large car park at the entrance to the abbey.

There is barely a town in France without a *petit train* (road-going tourists' train) these days, and Souillac is no exception. The Grand Hôtel is a fine place to stop for refreshment, either at its pavement café or in its ornate dining-room; there are street markets on Wednesdays and Saturdays and some good shops on the main road and in the Old Quarter; and Souillac has two unusual museums, the **Musée de l'Automate (**devoted to mechanical toys) and the **Musée des Attelages de la Belle Époque (**devoted to horse-drawn carriages). The Café de Paris was the wartime haunt of refugee Surrealists and Dadaists. Nowadays, the town always seems to be full of English visitors, partially because it is an obvious

Souillac's churches

With its domes and Byzantine styling, Souillac's **abbey church** has echoes of St-Front at Périgueux. The interior is a nice study in contrasts, with elaborate Romanesque carving above the west door which gives entrance to a plain, rather severe nave. The exterior is best viewed from a large paved area between the car park and the main street, where we can see five pentagonally-shaped chapels radiating from the curved east end of the church. The old parish church of **St-Martin**, which stood close by the abbey, was destroyed in the Wars of Religion. All that remains is a belfry with a huge gash in one side.

Abbey church, Souillac

stopping point on the route to Rocamadour, but also because there is a campsite nearby used by Eurocamp and the Caravan Club.

Martel

From Souillac, we take the D703 for **Martel**. The road passes under a tall and elegant viaduct and then under a newer road bridge. Martel, known as the 'Town of Seven Towers', has a wonderful medieval profile.

We can leave our car in one of the many shaded parking places on the long, straight avenue that runs alongside the old fortifications and set off on foot to explore this attractive town. In the Old Town, we find nice restaurants, a variety of shops, a market square with a splendid market hall, a number of old shop fronts, some quaint courtyards, lots of towers and a church that looks like a fortress. Architectural gems include: the **Hôtel de la Raymondie**, now the Town Hall, which has turrets, a belfry and a façade with quatrefoil window decorations; the **Maison Fabri**, former home

Above: Carennac from the bridge

Below: Old shop front, Martel

Summer idyll

During the 1960s and 70s, the influential gallery owner and art dealer John Kasmin and his wife Jane were in the habit of renting the eight-bedroomed château at Carennac as a summer retreat. Kasmin's famous artist friends, such as Howard Hodgkin, Patrick Procktor and David Hockney, together with the sculptor Anthony Caro, often drove down to join them for idyllic summer breaks.

The hosts slept in a very grand bed and the children had a great time sleeping in sleeping bags in the château's tower. Kasmin used a vast kitchen range to produce meals which were consumed by the guests at a long table in the garden. When they were not playing chess on the terrace, Hockney and Procktor produced beautiful works of art. Hockney concentrated on making carefully-executed coloured pencil sketches of leeks, red peppers, limes, pineapples and courgettes (zucchini) and some pen drawings, including one of Kasmin lying on the grand bed with book in hand. Procktor, meanwhile, painted a number of pictures in watercolours, a medium rarely used by Hockney. Inspired by his observation of his friend at work, Hockney decided to try his hand at watercolour painting. He did produce a few works, but he was so dissatisfied with the results that he gave his watercolour paints to Procktor.

of Henry Short Coat; and the **Hotel de la Monnaie**, where coins were once minted.

The town is said to have been founded by Charles Martel, conqueror of the Saracens, and its crest features three hammers, apparently Charles' favourite weapons. In the thirteenth century, Martel was made a 'free town', which entitled it to tax exemptions and the right to produce its own money. Although the place suffered in the Hundred Years' War and in the Wars of Religion and then went into something of a decline, it remains a thriving market centre and a remarkable medieval survival.

From Martel, we follow the N140 down to the Dordogne river, where there is a suspension bridge and a superb view of the village of **Gluges**, whose tall, white church tower rises like a limestone pinnacle between two cliffs.

CARENNAC

We now follow the D43, passing on our way through the very narrow streets of **Floirac** (beware!). The road takes us through thick woods near the south bank of the Dordogne. At the heart of the woods, we come unexpectedly upon **Carennac**, a village which looks exactly like a small medieval city in a storybook illustration. Notwithstanding the outstanding beauty of places such as St-Jean-de-Côle, Monpazier, Limeuil, Beynac, La Roque-Gageac and Domme, Carennac is my own favourite Dordogne village. The consistent use of warm brown stone and mellow roof-tiles gives the place a wonderful homogeneity and its many towers give the village an urban feel. The visual symphony that is Carennac builds to a dramatic crescendo at its very core, where a sixteenth century château and the **Église St-Pierre** combine to form one large fortified pile of buildings. When we walk through an archway into this seemingly secret place, we come to a flight of steps which leads to a magnificently-carved **Romanesque Portal**, possibly fashioned by sculptors from Toulouse. The stone of the doorway is so bright that the portal seems to emit its own unearthly light. The interior of the church has some elaborately carved capitals and there are interesting cloisters, galleries and a chapter house with a celebrated entombment, but there is nothing to compare with that portal!

The village of Carennac was founded in the tenth century around a deanery and priory. Although the deanery suffered during the Revolution and some of the village buildings have fallen into decay over the years, Carennac is being sensitively restored. Many houses have been renovated but the settlement has not been artificially face-lifted or spoilt in any way.

There is a nice fishing jetty by the Dordogne and there are riverside walks through the most tranquil landscapes imaginable.

On the rough path that leads down to the river, there is a wonderfully

Halfway to hell

It is quite common for large natural chasms to be given legendary associations with the Devil. The deeper the hole, the more bizarre the story.

There are several versions of devilish connections with the Gouffre de Padirac. One rather appealing story has the Devil using the chasm as a sort of pleasure resort or resting place on his travels between hell and the ground. Another version, probably inspired by marks on the ground at the entrance to the Padirac chasm, tells of a meeting between St Martin and Satan. According to this story, St Martin was riding along on his donkey when the animal came to an abrupt halt. Satan appeared on the scene carrying a sack-load of souls which he offered to surrender to St Martin if the saint and his donkey could jump across a ravine that he had created by stamping his foot on the ground. The saint and his animal duly obliged and Satan fled down his hole to hell.

The marks at the entrance to the cave are said to have been made by the donkey's hooves.

Above: Gluges

picturesque tower where, it is claimed, Fénelon wrote *Les Aventures de Télémarque*, a chronicle of the supposed exploits of Ulysses' son. Whether the author really used the tower as his study is open to question, but the image of a writer scribbling away in his tower is a romantic notion that is entirely appropriate in this most romantic of villages.

Fénelon was the Prior of Carennac for fifteen years. He is said to have written the story of Télémarque for the amusement of Louis XIV's grandson, to whom he was appointed tutor. When his novel was published, it was interpreted as a criticism of Louis' court, and Fénelon was banished to Cambrai.

DETOUR TO GOUFFRE DE PADIRAC

If we retrace our route to the N140, we can drop south to the crossroads with the D673. Rocamadour lies to the right, but we can turn left for a short detour to the **Gouffre de Padirac**, a vast chasm used, according to legend, by Satan, as a place where he could relax half-way between hell and ground level. The cave, which had been used by local people as a hide-out during the Hundred Years' War and the Wars of Religion, was explored in 1889 by Edouard Martel, who discovered a vast cave network and a subterranean river. Visitors are taken, via lifts, over 200ft (160m) below the surface to view

For Whom the Bell Tolls

As the eldest son of Henry Plantagenet, Henry Court-Mantel, otherwise known as Henry Short Coat, was entitled to an allowance and a share in his father's considerable French territorial possessions. However, Short Coat was disloyal and the king cut off his allowance and bestowed his favours on one of his other sons, Richard the Lionheart. In reprisal and in an attempt to gain power and money, Short Coat went on the rampage, plundering the treasure houses of south-west France. After his most sacrilegious act, the plundering of the oratory at Rocamadour, he retreated to Martel where, it is said, he became repentant. When Short Coat found that he had contracted a life-threatening fever, he sent for his father to ask for forgiveness. The king, who was too busy fighting to come along to Martel himself, sent a messenger with a pardon. This duly arrived before Short Coat expired.

A more fanciful version has Henry Short Coat filled with repentance when the bells of Rocamadour rang out on their own accord to signify the Virgin's anger. When the messenger arrived at Martel, he found Short Coat so overcome with remorse that he had placed himself on a bed of cinders. A heavy wooden cross lay on his chest.

Below: Romanesque porch, Carennac

Below: The steps at Rocamadour

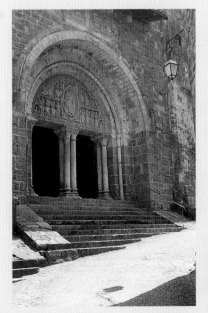

the wonders of the cave system. The return journey is by a combination of boat and lift.

ROCAMADOUR

After returning to the crossroads on the N140, we take the road westwards to **Rocamadour**. If we stop at the *table d'orientation*, we can look across a wide, deep valley to a village which is so fantastic that it seems unreal. As we have seen, there are many clinging villages in the Dordogne region, but this one is the most gravity-defying of them all, for many of Rocamadour's buildings are actually built on the face of a vertical cliff. The sun always seems to be in the wrong direction for good photographs of the village from this vantage point, but it is simply not necessary to have a souvenir photograph in order to keep this amazing scene in the mind.

We enter the village down a steep road that passes under a rock tunnel. There is ample parking at the foot of the settlement and *petits trains* leave the car park for the village at ten-minute intervals.

If you can stomach the commercialism, Rocamadour is a feast of wonders. The massive **fort** at the foot of the cliff once housed the visiting pilgrims and the **Basilique St-Saveur** occupies an incredible location on the cliff-side that towers above the main street, with the rock-face forming one wall of the church. The famous steps lead up the cliff to the restored **Chapelle Notre Dame**, on the site of the hermit's oratory. The carved figure of the Black Virgin stands on the altar, with the infant Jesus, eerily carved with an adult face, sitting on her knee. A thousand year-old bell, which supposedly rings on its own accord when miracles are about to occur, hangs from the ceiling.

Those who feel disinclined to walk up the steps, let alone climb on their hands and knees (see Rocamadour's History), can take a lift to the summit of the cliff, from where there are wonderful views of the valley and the roof-tops of Rocamadour.

There is a profusion of museums and visitor centres in and around the town. The **Musée d'Art Sacré**, dedicated to the composer Francis Poulenc, who is said to have experienced a revelation on a visit to Rocamadour in 1936 which inspired him to write a Litany to the Black Virgin, contains paintings, statues and relics collected from the treasuries of many churches.

Rocamadour's other attractions are of a very different nature. The **Musée du Jouet Ancien Automobile**, near the town gate, contains a collection of toy cars; the **Jardin des Papillons**, just outside the town, houses hundreds of colourful butterflies and the **Rocher des Aigles**, high above the town, is home to a number of birds of prey, which are flown at regular intervals through the day. On the road to Figeac, there is a **Euro Mini Land**, with cleverly animated scenes, and the **Forêt des Singes**, which houses more than 100 monkeys and apes.

Rocamadour is especially splendid after dark, when the whole village is floodlit. It is possible to return to Souillac and Sarlat by taking a long, winding road through dense woods west of

Rocamadour's history

Rocamadour became a pilgrimage centre in the twelfth century after the uncorrupted corpse of a man was discovered below the threshold of the Chapelle Notre-Dame. When the body of the man, said to have been a hermit who had hollowed out an oratory in the rock, was removed and placed by the altar of the chapel, miracles began to occur. Henry Plantagenet set a trend when he knelt before the Virgin to give thanks after recovering from illness during a visit here. Thousands of pilgrims came to venerate Our Lady of Rocamadour during the Middle Ages and heretics were also sent here by tribunals in order to receive absolution. Over 200 stone steps lead up the cliff face to the charred shrine known as the 'Black Virgin' and the heretics were required to climb them on their knees whilst bound in chains.

Rocamadour eventually went into a relative decline and suffered, like so many other places in the Dordogne, from the ravages of war, but it was revived as a pilgrimage centre during the nineteenth century, when its churches and ecclesiastical centres were rebuilt.

Today, Rocamadour is one of the most visited places in France and it unashamedly prostitutes its charms. The main street is teeming with restaurants, cafés, trinket shops and outlets for *foie gras* and truffles. Already feeling somewhat put off by the memory of all the commercialism I had witnessed on a previous visit, I was well and truly switched off Rocamadour on my most recent visit when a shopkeeper came out of his premises to prevent me taking a photograph of his shop front. My protestation that France is supposed to be part of the 'Free World' made no impression on him.

the village, but this route is somewhat intimidating at night, so it is advisable to head for to the N140 for the return journey.

Our visit to the villages of Carennac and Rocamadour is an appropriate finale to our tour of Périgord, for these two settlements represent the two contrasting faces of the Dordogne region. Carennac is quiet, unassuming and hidden in the woods, but very beautiful; Rocamadour is loud and brash, but incredibly spectacular. It is inevitable that a region where man and nature have combined in such dramatic fashion should contain some overcrowded and commercialised show places, but the Dordogne is also full of surprises and hidden gems. All of these attractions, be they showy or modest, famous or little-known, are far too good to miss!

Additional Information

The Purple Périgord

Accommodation

Hotels

For hotels in the base town of Le Bugue see the Purple Périgord chapter. Most of the hotels on the Heart of the Dordogne Tour are in superb locations and some have rooms with spectacular views. When booking, it is worth asking for 'a room with a view'.

If you are very keen to see the main show caves near Les Eyzies or Lascaux II, near Montignac, there is a strong case for staying near these places. Tickets have to be bought early in the morning to ensure a visit on your chosen day.

Beynac

Hôtel Bonnet ★★
☎ 05 5329 5001
21 rooms, riverside terrace.

★★ Hôtel du Château
☎ 05 5329 5013
On the way to the castle, 18 rooms.

Hôtel Maleville ★★
☎ 05 5329 5006
13 rooms.

Hôtel Pontet ★★
☎ 05 5335 2683
13 rooms.

Carennac

Auberge du Vieux Quercy ★★
☎ 06 510 9659
Swimming pool.

Hostellerie Fénelon ★★
☎ 06 510 9646
Swimming pool.

Carsac-Aillac

Le Relais de Touron ★★
☎ 05 5328 1670
12 rooms, Swimming pool.

Hôtel Delpeyrat
☎ 05 53281043
13 rooms.

Domme

Hôtel l'Esplanade ★★★
☎ 05 53283141
25 rooms, some have spectacular views of the Dordogne countryside.

Le Relais du Chevalier ★★
★★ 05 5328 3388
6 rooms.

Les 4 Vents ★★
☎ 05 5331 5757
20 rooms.

Hôtel Lou Cardil ★
☎ 05 5328 3892
10 rooms, nice inner courtyard.

★ Nouvel Hôtel
☎ 05 5328 3867
17 rooms.

Les Eyzies-de-Tayac

Hôtel du Centenaire ★★★
☎ 05 5306 9718
19 rooms, swimming pool, sauna and gym.

Le CroMagnon ★★★
☎ 05 5306 9706
22 rooms, swimming pool.

Hôtel des Glycines ★★★
☎ 05 5306 9707
25 rooms, swimming pool.

Hôtel du Centre ★★
☎ 05 5306 9713
19 rooms.

Hôtel de France **
☎ 05 5306 9723
25 rooms, swimming pool.

Hôtel Moulin de Beaune **
☎ 05 5306 9433
20 rooms.

Hôtel des Roches **
☎ 05 5306 9659
41 rooms, swimming pool.

Hôtel des Falaises-Tourisme
☎ 05 5306 9935
14 rooms.

Gluges
Hôtel des Falaises ***
☎ 06 5373 359
Nice gardens and on a spectacular site.

Auberge de l'Isle
☎ 06 5322 201. Swimming pool and terrace.

Martel
Hôtel Falaises *
☎ 06 5373 359

Montignac
Château de Puy Robert ****
☎ 05 5351 9213
38 rooms, swimming pool; hotel is a château set in a 20-acre (8-hectare) park.

La Roserie ***
☎ 05 5350 5392
14 rooms, swimming pool.

Le Relais du Soleil d'Or ***
☎ 05 5351 8022
32 rooms, swimming pool.

Le Lascaux **
☎ 05 5351 8281
14 rooms.

Rocamadour
Beau Site ***
☎ 06 5336 308
With 4-posters.

Sainte-Marie **
☎ 06 5336 307
Excellent views.

Hôtel du Roc **
☎ 06 5336 243

Hôtel du Globe **
☎ 06 5336 773
In the centre.

Panoramic **
☎ 06 533 6306
Swimming pool.

Below: St-Cyprien, the village and abbey church

Additional Information

La Roque-Gageac

Hôtel de la Belle Étoile ★★
☎ 05 5329 5144
14 rooms.

Hôtel Gardette ★★
☎ 05 5329 5158
15 rooms.

Hôtel le Périgord ★★
☎ 05 5328 3655
40 rooms, swimming pool, tennis.

St-Amand-de-Coly

Hôtel Gardette-Tourisme
☎ 05 5351 6850
6 rooms.

St-Cyprien

Hôtel de l'Abbaye ★★★
☎ 05 5329 2048
24 rooms, swimming pool.

Hôtel de la Terrasse ★★
☎ 05 5329 2169
17 rooms.

St-Geniès

Le Relais des Touristes ★
☎ 05 5328 9760
12 rooms.

St-Léon-sur-Vézère

Relais de St Léon ★★
☎ 05 5350 7447
20 rooms, swimming pool, idyllic location.

St-Vincent-de-Cosse

Le Coustaty
☎ 05 5329 5529
10 rooms, swimming pool.

Salignac-Eyvignes

La Terrasse ★★
☎ 05 5328 8038
14 rooms, swimming pool.
Souillac

Bellevue ★★
☎ 06 5327 823
Swimming pool.

Hostellerie La Roserie ★★
☎ 06 5378 269
Swimming pool.

La Vieille Auberge ★★
☎ 06 5327 943

Auberge du Puits ★
☎ 06 5378 032

Tamniès

Laborderie ★★
☎ 05 5329 6859
39 rooms, swimming pool.

Vézac

Manoir de Rochecourbe ★★★
☎ 05 5331 0984

Le Relais des Cinq Châteaux ★★
☎ 05 5330 3072
10 rooms, swimming pool.

Hôtel l'Oustal ★★
☎ 05 5329 5421
20 rooms, swimming pool.

Vitrac

Domaine de Rochebois ★★★★
☎ 05 3283 304
40 rooms, Swimming pool and 9-hole golf course.

Burg ★★
☎ 05 3283 329
Swimming pool.

Hôtel la Treille ★★
☎ 05 5328 3319
8 rooms.

Plaisance ★★
☎ 05 5328 3304
Swimming pool and canoe rentals.

Camping

As with hotels, there are many campsites in this area, all well located in lovely locations and near to the sights.

Much of the Pilgrimage Tour has taken us away from Périgord and into the Lot, but a selection of convenient campsites is given at Carsac-Aillac, Rocamadour, Souillac and Vitrac.

For the base town of Le Bugue see the Purple Périgord chapter.

Beynac
Camping Le Capeyrou ★★
☎ 05 5329 5495
100 emplacements, swimming pool.

Carsac-Aillac
Camping Aqua-Viva ★★★★
☎ 05 5331 4600
160 emplacements, well-equipped, used by the Caravan Club.

Camping Plein Air des Bories ★★★
☎ 05 5328 1567
110 emplacements.

Castelnaud
Camping Lou Castel ★★★
☎ 05 5329 8924
57 emplacements, swimming pool.

Cénac
Camping le Pech de Caumont ★★★
☎ 05 5328 2163
100 emplacements, swimming pool.

Cénac Plage ★
☎ 05 5328 3191
Municipal site, 112 emplacements.

Domme
Camping Le Perpetuum ★★★
☎ 05 5328 3518
120 emplacements, swimming pool.

La Rivière de Domme ★★
☎ 05 5328 3346
50 emplacements, swimming pool.

Le Bosquet ★★
☎ 05 5328 3739
60 emplacements, swimming pool.

Camping Le Brat ★
☎ 05 5328 3420
30 emplacements.

Le Moulin de Caudon ★
☎ 05 5331 0369
60 emplacements.

Les Eyzies-de-Tayac
Le Mas ★★★★
☎ 05 5329 6806
136 emplacements, swimming pool, tennis.

Le Périgord ★★★
☎ 05 5354 5957

La Rivière ★★★
☎ 05 5306 9714
120 emplacements, swimming pool, tennis.

Montignac
Le Bleufond ★★
☎ 05 5351 8373
90 emplacements, swimming pool.

Rocamadour
Relais du Campeur L'Hospitalet
☎ 06 533 6328
With a swimming pool.

La Roque-Gageac
Camping Beaurivage ★★★
☎ 05 5328 3205
199 emplacements, swimming pool, tennis.

Camping Le Lauzier ★★
☎ 05 5329 5459
66 emplacements, swimming pool.

Camping Verte Rive ★
☎ 05 5328 3004
60 emplacements.

Rouffignac
Cantegrel ★
☎ 05 5305 4830
110 emplacements, swimming pool, tennis.

Additional Information

St-Amand-de-Coly
Hamelin Périgord Vacances *
☎ 05 5351 6064
44 emplacements, swimming pool.

Les Malenies *
☎ 05 5350 8157

St-Cyprien
Camping du Garrit **
☎ 05 5329 2056
Municipal site, 75 emplacements.

St-Léon-sur-Vézère
Le Paradis ****
☎ 05 5350 7264
200 emplacements, swimming pool, tennis.

Camping Municipal *
☎ 05 5350 7316

St-Vincent-de-Cosse
Camping Tiradou ***
☎ 05 5330 3073
60 emplacements, swimming pool.

Tamniès
Le Pont de Mazerat *****
☎ 05 5329 1495

Tursac
Le Vézère Périgord ******
☎ 05 5306 9631
103 emplacements, swimming pool, tennis.

Petit train, Souillac

La Ferme du Pelou ★★
☎ 05 5306 9817
65 emplacements.

Le Pigeonnier ★★
☎ 05 53069690
25 emplacements, swimming pool.

Le Bouyssau ★
☎ 05 53069808
20 emplacements.

L'Espinasse ★
☎ 05 53069823

Vézac
Camping Les Deux Vallées ★★★
☎ 05 53295355
100 emplacements, swimming pool.

Camping La Cabane ★★
☎ 05 53295228
98 emplacements, swimming pool.

Camping la Plage ★
☎ 05 53295083
83 emplacements.

Vitrac
Camping Soleil Plage ★★★★
☎ 05 53283333
199 emplacements, swimming pool, tennis.

Camping La Bouysse ★★★
☎ 05 53283305
160 emplacements, swimming pool, tennis.

Camping Clos Bernard ★★
☎ 05 53283344
95 emplacements.

Camping La Sagne ★
☎ 05 53310096
30 emplacements.

Activity Centres
Beynac
Barge Trips
☎ 05 5328 5115
Open: 10am–1pm, 2–6pm. Trips last for 50 minutes and leave every 30 minutes.

Enjoying a river trip, Beynac

Carsac-Aillac
Canoeing
Aqua-Viva
☎ 05 5359 2109

Castelnaud
Horse Riding
La Vallée de Châteaux
☎ 05 5329 5186

Canoeing
Kayak Club
☎ 05 5329 1765

Cénac
Canoeing
Randonnée Dordogne
☎ 05 5328 2201

Cénac Périgord Loisirs
☎ 05 5329 9969

Canoë Sioux
☎ 05 5328 3081

Additional Information

Domme
Canoeing
Espace Canoë
☎ 05 5359 4221

Les-Eyzies-de-Tayac
Canoeing
Basse des 3 Drapeaux
☎ 05 5306 9189

Animation Vézère
☎ 05 5306 9292

Montignac
Canoeing
☎ 05 5351 8260

Animation Vézère
☎ 05 5351 9114

Les 7 Rives
☎ 05 5350 1926

La Roque-Gageac
Boat Trips
Les Caminades
☎ 05 5329 4095
A 1-hour trip operates from Mar to Oct
between 9.30am–6pm.

Les Norberts
☎ 05 5329 4044
A 1-hour trip. Boats leave every 30
minutes, 10am–6pm in Jul and Aug;
10am–5pm in Apr, May, Jun and Sep
and Oct.

Ballooning
Montgolfière du Périgord
☎ 05 5328 1858

Canoeing
Canoë Dordogne
☎ 05 5329 5850

Canoës Vacances
☎ 05 5328 1707

La-Roque-St-Christophe
Horse Riding
Viseur Michel
☎ 05 5306 9383

St-Léon-sur-Vézère
Canoeing
Aventure Plein Air
☎ 05 5350 6771

Tamniès
Horse Riding
Le Gîte de Favard
☎ 05 5329 6862

Vitrac (near Sarlat)
Canoeing
Canoës Loisirs
☎ 05 5328 2343

Soleil Plage
☎ 05 5328 3333

Golf
Golf Domaine de Rochebois
☎ 05 5331 5280.

Horse Riding
L'Étrier de Vitrac
☎ 05 5359 3431

Attractions

Beynac
Château
☎ 05 5329 5040
Open: mid-Mar to mid-Nov 10am–12
noon, 12.15–1.45pm. 1-hour long guided
tours every 30 minutes. Independent
visits 12.15–1.45pm.

Carennac
Cloisters
☎ 05 6510 9701
1-hour guided tour. Open: 10am–1pm,
2–7pm May to mid-Sep; 10.30am–
12.30pm, 2–6pm Mar to Apr and mid-
Sep to Oct.

Castelnaud
Château
☎ 05 5331 3000
Open: 9am–8pm Jul and Aug; 10am–
7pm May, Jun and Sep; 10am–6pm
Mar, Apr, Oct and early Nov; 2–5pm
late Nov to mid-Feb. Night spectacle
at 8.30pm and 10.15pm in summer
months except Sat and Sun.

Domme
Caves
☎ 05 5328 3709
30-minute guided tour. Open: daily
9am–7pm Jul, Aug; 9.30am–12 noon,
2–6pm Apr, May, Jun, Sep; 2–5pm Feb,
Mar and Oct.

Musée des Arts et Traditions Populaires
☎ 05 5328 3709
Open: 10am–12.30pm, 2–6pm Apr to
Sep.

Eyrignac
Gardens
☎ 05 5328 9971
Open: 10.30am–12.30pm, 2.30pm–
nightfall Jan to Mar; 10am–12.30pm,
2–7pm Jun to Sep; 10.30am–12 noon,
2.30pm-nightfall from Oct to Dec.

Les Eyzies-de-Tayac
Abri du Cap Blanc
☎ 05 5359 2174
30-minute guided tour. Open: 9.30am–
7pm Jul and Aug; 10am–12 noon,
2–4pm Apr to Jun, Sep to Oct.

Grotte de Combarelles
☎ 05 5308 0094
Open: 9am–12 noon, 2–6pm April to
September; 10am–12 noon, 2–4pm Oct
to Mar. In high season tickets for morning
visits must by purchased by 9am and
those for afternoon visits by 2pm.

Grotte de Font-de-Gaume
☎ 05 5308 0094
Open: 9am–12 noon, 2–6pm Apr to
Sep; 10am–12 noon, 2–5pm Mar and
Oct; 10am–12 noon, 2–4pm from Nov
to Feb. Tickets should be bought in the
morning.

Abri du Poisson
☎ 05 5306 9703
Book at Grotte de Font-de-Gaume,
opening times as above.

Grotte du Grand Roc
☎ 05 5306 9703
Open: 9am–7pm Jul and Aug; 9am–12
noon, 2–6pm mid-Mar to Jun and Sep to
mid-Nov.

Musée National de Préhistoire
☎ 05 5306 9703.
Closed on Tuesdays. Open: 9.30am–
12 noon, 2–6pm Apr to Nov; 9.30am–12
noon, 2–5pm Dec to Mar.

Musée de la Spéléologie
☎ 05 5329 6842
Closed on Sat. Open: 9am–12 noon,
2–6pm Jul and Aug.

Fénelon
Château
☎ 05 5329 8145
Guided tours last 1 hour. Open:
9.30am–7pm Jun to Sep; 10am–12
noon, 2–6pm rest of the year.

Lascaux
See Montignac.

Additional Information

Losse

Château

☎ 05 5350 8008

Open: 10am–7pm Jun to Aug; 10am–12 noon, 1–6pm Easter to May and in Sep; 11am–5pm at other times.

Martel

Musée de la Raymondie

☎ 06 537 3003

Open: 10am–12 noon, 2–6.30pm Jul and Aug.

Les Milandes

Château

☎ 05 5359 3121

Open: 9am–7pm Jun, Jul and Aug; 10am–6pm Apr, May, Sep; 2–5pm rest of year.

Montignac

Lascaux II

☎ 05 5351 9503

Open: 9.30am–7pm Jul and Aug; 10am–12 noon, 2–5.30pm rest of year. Closed on Mon. Tickets must be bought from the Information Centre in Montignac.

Espace Cro-Magnon, Le Thot

☎ 05 5350 7044

Double tickets for Lascaux II and the museum can be purched from the Information Centre in Montignac. Opening times as above.

Musée Eugène le Roy

Open: 9.30am–7pm Jul and Aug; 10am–12 noon, 2–5.30pm Feb to Jun and Sep to Dec. Closed Mon. Tickets from Information Centre in Montignac.

Padirac

Gouffre de Padirac

☎ 05 6533 6456

Open: 8.30am–12 noon, 2–6.30pm Jul; 8am–7pm in Aug; 9am–12 noon, 2–6pm rest of year between Apr and mid-Oct

Puymartin

Château

☎ 05 5359 2997

Open: 10am–12 noon, 2–6.30pm Apr to Oct; closes at 6pm Apr, May and late Sep.

Rocamadour

Euro Mini Land

☎ 05 6533 6456

By rail at intervals throughout the day. Times change; check on leaflets.

Forêt des Singes

☎ 05 6533 6272 or 05 6533 6328

Open: 10am–7pm Jul and Aug; 10am–12 noon, 2–6pm Palm Sunday to Jun and Sep to mid-Nov.

Grotte des Merveilles

☎ 05 6533 6792

Open: 9am–12 noon, 1.30–7pm Jul and Aug; 10am–12 noon, 2–6pm rest of year between Palm Sunday and All Saints' Day.

Jardin des Papillons

Open: 9am–7pm Jul and Aug; 10am–12 noon, 2–6pm Apr to Jun and Sep to Oct.

Musée d'Art Sacré

☎ 05 6533 6329

(Francis Poulenc Treasure Museum)
Open: 9am–12 noon, 2–6pm Palm Sunday to All Saints' Day.

Musée du Jouet Ancien Automobile
☎ 05 6533 6683
Open: 8am–8pm Easter to Sep.

Ramparts
☎ 05 6533 6329
Open: 9am–7pm Jul and Aug; 9am–12 noon, 2–7pm rest of year between Palm Sunday and All Saints' Day.

Rocher des Aigles
☎ 05 6533 6545
Open: 10am–12 noon, 2–7pm Palm Sunday to mid-Nov. Demonstrations in high season at 11am, 1pm, 2.30pm, 3.30pm, 4.30pm, 5.30pm.

La Roque-St-Christophe
Cave Shelters
☎ 05 5350 7045
45-minute guided tour available 10am–7pm Jul and Aug; 10am–6pm Mar to Jun and Sept to Nov; 11am–5pm Dec and Feb.

Rouffignac
Grotte de Rouffignac
☎ 05 5305 4171
Open: 9–11.30am, 2–6pm Jul to mid-Sep; 10–11.30am, 2–5pm Palm Sunday to mid-Jun and mid-Sep to end of Oct.

Musée de l'Automobile
☎ 05 5305 9501
Open: 2–7pm Easter to Sep, but also 10am–12 noon mid-Jul to Aug.

St-Amand-de-Coly
Church
Open: 9am–7pm throughout the year

Salignac-Eyvignes
Château
☎ 05 5328 8006
Open: 10.30am–1pm, 2–6pm, except Tue in Jul and Aug; 2–6pm at Easter, second half of Jun and first half of Sep; closed Tue.

Souillac
Musée des Attelages de la Belle Époque
☎ 05 6537 0775
Open: 10am–12 noon, 3–7pm Jul to Sep.

Musée de l'Automate
☎ 05 6537 0707
Open: 10am–7pm Jul and Aug; 2–5pm Nov to Mar, closed Mon, Tue; 10am–12 noon, 3–6pm Apr, May, Oct, closed Mon.

Tursac
Pré-histo Parc
☎ 05 5350 7319 or 05 5306 9676
Open: 9am–7pm May to Sep; 9am–12 noon, 2–6pm Mar, Apr, Oct, Nov.

Eating Out
The exquisite perched villages in the heart of the Dordogne are perfect locations for eating out. There is a very good choice of restaurants.

Les Eyzies, the honeypot for the swarms of tourists who visit this region, has a good selection of restaurants. Montignac, near the Lascaux caves, and the beautiful village of St-Léon-sur-Vézère are two other good venues for dining out.

Beynac
Bonnet
☎ 05 5329 8374
Has a splendid riverside terrace. Pastry with truffles is a speciality.

Maleville
☎ 055329 5006
Also on the riverside, has meals ranging from reasonable to expensive in price. Madame Maleville is carrying on a family tradition.

Le Relais des Cinq Châteaux
☎ 05 5330 3072
Near Vézac, is very popular. It offers good value for money and a vegetarian menu.

Additional Information

Carennac

Auberge de Vieux Quercy

☎ 05 6510 9659

Has an excellent menu at prices which are not excessive.

Hostellerie Fénelon

☎ 05 6510 9646

Also offers good regional dishes at moderate prices.

Carsac-Aillac

Hotel Delpeyrat

☎ 05 5328 1043

A member of the Logis de France chain, has a reasonably-priced restaurant.

Domme

L'Esplanade

☎ 0553283141

Occupies a superb cliff-top setting. The truffle dishes are good, but not cheap.

Les Eyzies

Restaurant Le Centenaire

☎ 05 5306 9718

Is a celebrated restaurant with two Michelin stars. Regional dishes are concocted from fresh local produce.

Restaurant Le Châteaubriant

☎ 05 5335 0611

At the heart of the Capital of Prehistory, also offers regional dishes fashioned from local produce.

Hotel Cro-Magnon

☎ 05 5306 9706

Has one Michelin star and offers diners the chance to enjoy regional specialities in a particularly attractive dining room.

Restaurant de Laugerie Basse

☎ 05 5306 9791

Situated next to the Grotte du Grand Roc, has a terrace overlooking the Vézère. Traditional cuisine is offered at a range of prices.

La Métairie

☎ 05 532 96532

4 miles (6.5km) from Les Eyzies, offers cheap, but excellent meals in a rustic setting.

Montignac

Le Lascaux

☎ 05 5351 8281

Serves up authentic Périgord dishes at reasonable prices in a pleasant restaurant.

Le Périgord

☎ 05 5350 5631

In the Rue Tourny, also offers local dishes at very acceptable prices.

Rocamadour

Beau Site

☎ 05 6533 6308

Located in a medieval building, has excellent fish dishes.

Château de Roumegouse

05 6533 6381

Just outside Rocamadour, has high quality Perigord dishes at prices to match.

Sainte-Marie

☎ 05 6533 6307

Has a very well recommended restaurant.

La Roque-Gageac

La Plume d'Oie

☎ 05 5329 5705

Has local cuisine at reasonable prices.

Les Prés Gaillardou
☎ 05 5359 6789
Offers good meals in a rustic setting.

St-Chamassy
Auberge la Veille Cure
☎ 05 5307 2424
Between Le Bugue and Soirac, is recommended by the locals.

St-Léon-sur-Vézère
Auberge du Pont
☎ 05 5350 7307
In this most beautiful of villages, has good regional cuisine.

Souillac
L'Ajoupa
☎ 05 6532 2211
Has a restaurant nicely set around a pool feature.

Shopping

All the villages on the Heart of the Dordogne Tour have excellent outlets for souvenirs, crafts and local products. The markets are not to be missed, if you can park!

Les Eyzies provides plenty of opportunities for buying local produce, fossils and souvenirs. There is an Intermarché supermarket on the road into Montignac

Souillac is a good general shopping centre. Souillac and Martel have good markets and Rocamadour is full of souvenirs. There are outlets for truffles at Souillac and Rocamadour.

Market Days

Cénac – Tuesday
Domme – Thursday
Les Eyzies – Monday
Martel – Wednesday and Saturday
Montignac – Wednesday
St-Cyprien – Sunday
Souillac – Wednesday and Friday

Supermarkets

There is a Champion supermarket at St Cyprien.There are Casino and Leclerc supermarkets at Souillac

Syndicats d'Initiative

La Roque-Gageac ☎ 05 53291701
Rouffignac ☎ 05 53053903
St-Cyprien ☎ 05 53303609

Tourist Information Centres

Beynac	☎ 05 53294308
Carennac	☎ 06 5109701
Domme	☎ 05 53317100
Les Eyzies-de-Tayac	☎ 05 53069705
Martel	☎ 06 5373003
Montignac	☎ 05 53518260
Souillac	☎ 06 5378156
Rocamadour	☎ 06 5336259

Accommodation

A local selection from the huge range of accommodation available in the Dordogne is given at the end of each section. This includes both hotels and campsites.

A day spent in a desperate search for a suitable place to stay is an appalling waste of holiday time, so it is advisable to book in advance, especially in a highly popular tourist region like Périgord.

All holiday makers, whatever their preferences (be it hotel, bed & breakfast, tent, caravan, gîte or youth hostel), expect their accommodation to offer value for money and provide a good geographical base. The quality of accommodation and its location can make or break a holiday. For some people, the joy of visiting one of the most beautiful regions in France can be turned into misery by a week spent in the company of flowery wallpaper, or a stay on a campsite without English-style toilets, or time in a gîte which is in a spot which is so 'peaceful' that any recognised tourist attraction is half a day's drive away. It is difficult to check out flowery wallpaper in advance, but I would advise everyone planning a holiday in the Dordogne to spend a few hours pouring over brochures, maps and guide books (especially this one) before making a booking.

Details of accommodation of all kinds can be obtained from the **French Government Tourist Office**, 178 Piccadilly, London W1 (☎ 0207 4919 995) or from **Service de Réservation Loisirs** Accueil, 25 Rue Wilson, 2400 Périgueux (☎ 05 5335 5024), but it is advisable to book travel and accommodation as a single package through a reputable company or travel agent.

Camping and caravan sites

There are some excellent caravan and camping sites in the Dordogne, many with swimming pools, restaurants, evening entertainment and children's play areas. If you have a young family or if you are taking teenagers, who generally prefer socialising to sightseeing, go for one of these sites. If you want to drink an evening bottle of wine in your awning with just the clicking of crickets for company, rather than loud and insistent music, opt for a lower-rated site. However if you want reasonable facilities, including adequate numbers of shower units and a few English-style toilets, it is important to stick to sites which have a 4-star ranking.

The Caravan Club (☎ 01342 316 101) and the **Camping and Caravaning Club** (☎ 01203 422 010) will arrange packages, including channel crossing and insurance, for those people taking their own caravan or tent. I would advise anyone taking a caravan to the Dordogne to take an awning with them. Once you are set up on site, the caravan itself can be used simply as a kitchen and bedroom, with the awning serving as dining-room, bar and sun lounge. In my experience, this is an idyllic way to spend time in France. As I write this, I ache to be in my awning once again, reclining on a sun lounger with a glass in my hand! Details of campsites are given in the Additional Information guides at the end of each chapter.

Driving to a set-up tent or mobile home is a popular choice for many people. Companies such as **Eurocamp** (☎ 01606 787 878), **Key Camp** (☎ 0870 7000 123), Sunsites (☎ 01606 787 555), **Canvas Holidays** (☎ 01383 644 000) and **Eurosites** (☎ 0870 7510 000) provide for this option. They also supply on-site representatives, who will offer advice about local attractions and cater for your every need, and they offer attractive packages, including multiple site holidays. These companies only use campsites with good facilities, so their brochures are also a good source of suitable sites for people taking their own caravans to France.

Gîtes

Gîte accommodation is very popular with visitors to France, especially those people who like to share their holiday with another family or travel in a small party. Gîtes are commonly converted farm buildings in pleasant country locations. However, it is important to check exact locations on a detailed map, because some gîtes are in areas which are a little too remote!

Information on gîtes, including the brochure **Gîtes de France**, is available from the **French Tourist Office in Piccadilly** (☎ 0207 4919 995) and many are advertised in the Sunday broadsheet newspapers or in magazines such as **France** and **Living France**.

Packages, including travel and gîte accommodation, can be organised by many companies, including:

Magic of France	☎ 0208 7410 208
Bowhills	☎ 01489 878 567
Brittany Ferries	☎ 0990 143 537
Country Cottages in France	☎ 01282 445 005
French Affair	☎ 0207 3818 519
Crystal	☎ 01235 824 324
Just France	☎ 0208 7804 480
Meon	☎ 01730 230 370
Something Special	☎ 01992 557 711
Vacances en Campagne	☎ 08700 780 185

Hotels

The traditional family-run hotels are usually billed as Logis de France, Auberges de France or France Accueil. An annual handbook is obtainable from the French Government Tourist Office in London (see above). Many of these hotels are in pretty and convenient locations and are often very charming in themselves.

Modern hotel chains include Novôtel, Ibis, Climat, Mercure, Sofitel, and Campanile. It is important to remember that these are used by business people, so tourists may end up paying for facilities, such as faxes, computer and telephone links, which are not needed by anyone who really wants 'to get away from it all'.

Whilst it is preferable to book in advance, choosing an appropriate French hotel from a brochure is not easy. Star ratings are of limited help, because they are based on physical provision, including those facilities which are only important to business people, rather than quality of service. I would advise intending tourists to identify those facilities which are important to them before reading brochures. If these are not clearly listed in the brochures, it is necessary to check with the hotels themselves or ask a travel agent to do so.

Hotels with lifts almost always carry higher ratings, and hence higher room charges, but the provision of a lift may not be important to the fit and healthy or those who are happy to use exercise to work off the effects of a full meal. The existence of private parking facilities is a major consideration, especially in busy centres or for security reasons, but an extra charge may be involved. Some hotels offer free accommodation to young children sharing a room, others charge a 'nominal fee'. The presence of satellite TV will be essential for those people who cannot manage without their favourite 'soap opera', even during their annual break. And whilst we're thinking about soap, the provision of private bathrooms, showers or saunas is a high priority for many people. Bidets are usually provided, whether you want one or not!

Details of hotels are given in the Additional Information guides at the end of each chapter.

Refuges

Gîtes d'étape and refuges are very basic forms of shelter, with bunk beds and simple kitchen facilities. They are usually located close to GR walking routes or cycle trails. Details can be found in the Rando Guide, available from the **Comité National des Sentiers de la Grande Randonnée**, 64 Rue de Gergovie 75014 Paris (☎ 01 4545 3102).

Youth Hostels

If you want a cheap holiday and you are happy to accept dormitory accommodation and basic meals, youth hostels (auberges de jeunesse) are the answer. Some town-based hostels are located in unattractive areas, but others are ideally placed, close to walking routes or activity areas.

Information can be obtained from **YHA**, 14 Southampton Street, London WC2 or from **AYH,** PO Box 37613, Washington DC 20013.

Disabled visitors

Some tourist attractions have limited access for disabled visitors. A comprehensive list of facilities for disabled visitors and details of access arrangements is given in **Touristes quand même! Promenades en France pour les Voyageurs Handicapés**. This publication can be obtained fromthe **Comité National Français de Liaison pour Réadaptiondes Handicapés**, 38 Boulevard Respail, 75007, Paris.

Electricity

The French system operates on 220v ac, 50 Hertz. A few areas still use 110v ac. Round 2-pin plugs are in general use for sockets, so visitors will need to take with them a continental 2-pin adaptor.

Events

Many events, fairs and festivals take place in Dordogne towns and villages during the summer months. Major festivals include:

Bergerac
July & August   **Musique en Périgord** and **Festival du Périgord Pourpre**

Biron
July & August   **Festival du Périgord Pourpre**

Bourdeilles
Second week in September   **Sinfonia en Périgord**

Le Bugue
July & August   **Musique en Périgord**

Cadouin
July & August   **Festival du Périgord Pourpre**

Chancelade
Second week in September   **Sinfonia en Périgord**

Les Eyzies
July & August   **Musique en Périgord**

Monpazier
July & August   **Festival du Périgord Pourpre**

Montignac
Last week in July   **International Folklore Festival**

Périgueux
August   **International Mime Festival** (Mimos)
Late August, early September   **French Song Festival**
Second week in September   **Sinfonia en Périgord**

St-Jean-de-Côle
Second week in September   **Sinfonia en Périgord**

St-Léon-sur-Vézère
July & August   **Festival Musique du Périgord Noir**

Sarlat
Late July & early August   **Festival des Jeux du Théâtre**

Souillac
Third week in July   **Jazz Festival**

Above: Paper decorations

Left: Foie Gras

Right: Cycling in the Dordogne

Below: Still waters at Castelnaud

Health

British visitors should obtain a Form 111 from the Department of Health and Social Security. This ensures access to health services in France. Each member of the family must fill in an application form.

American and Canadian visitors will need to check the validity of their personal health insurances to ensure that they are adequately covered for their trip.

In an emergency, phone 19 or the local police station. Pharmacists always give very helpful advice and stock a very comprehensive range of products.

Remember to take with you sun-cream and applications to prevent mosquito bites.

Measurements

1 mile is equivalent to 1.6km, so a journey of 100 miles will be signed as 160km. In order to make a rough conversion of km to miles, multiply by 6 and divide by 10, so 100km is about 60 miles.

British people are now much more familiar with continental measurements of area, volume and weight. For the record, conversions are as follows:

2.2lb is equivalent to 1kg (1,000g)
1.75 pints is equivalent to 1l
1 gallon is equivalent to 4.5l
2.5 acres is equivalent to 1 hectare

Money

There is no restriction on the amount of money which can be taken into France, but visitors would be well advised to minimise the amount of cash they carry by taking Eurocheques and travellers' cheques and by using credit cards to pay for fuel and to pay bills at supermarkets and restaurants. Cards such as Access, Visa and American Express are widely accepted.

Banks are normally open from 9am to 12 noon and 2 to 4pm.

Outdoor Activities

The Dordogne has more outdoor activities than any region in France.

Boat trips

Pleasure boats, which operate from centres such as Bergerac, Beynac, Brantôme and La Roque-Gageac, provide a serene way of viewing beautiful river scenery and spectacular clinging villages, but they are very popular and advance booking may be necessary in high season. Details are given at the end of each chapter.

Canoeing

Canoeing is incredibly popular with holidaymakers in Périgord. Kayaks and canoes can be hired at waterside centres on a number of rivers, with the Dordogne and the Vézère being the most popular. The Dordogne has no less than 17 hire centres along its banks, the Vézère has 6, the Dronne has 3, L'Isle has 2 and

L'Auvézère has 2. Details of hire centres are given at the end of each chapter and information can also be found in the free Périgord Découvert guide which is available at all information centres. Stretches of water are classified, according to increasing difficulty, on a scale of 1 to 5. Life jackets are included in the hire charge, and hirers have the choice of 'jumping in at the deep end' or receiving tuition. Minibuses run between pick-up points along the rivers, so it is possible to design voyages of virtually any length.

The weir at Brantôme provides some fun and a safe challenge for beginners, and Limeuil, at the confluence of the Dordogne and Vézère rivers, and at the heart of some of the most scenic and safest stretches, is an ideal centre for families to hire canoes and kayaks.

For the more adventurous, rafts are available for hire, when and where conditions permit their use.

Centres include:

On the Dordogne: Carsac-Aillac, Castelnaud, Cénac; Domme, Lalinde, Limeuil, La Roque-Gageac, St-Laurent-des-Hommes, St-Vincent-de-Cosse, Vézac, Vitrac

On the Vézère: Le Bugue, Les Eyzies, Limeuil, Montignac, St-Léon-sur-Vézère

On the Dronne: Bourdeilles, Brantôme, Ribérac

on the Isle: Périgueux

Details are given in the Additional Information guides at the end of each chapter.

Climbing and caving

There are many tempting opportunities for climbing and caving on and in the limestone rocks of the Dordogne region, but these activities are best pursued through organisations or in organised groups. The Loisirs Accueil office in Périgueux (☎ 05 5335 5024) has details of organised climbing and caving opportunities and the **Comité Départmental de Spéléologie, Dordogne** (☎ 05 5331 2730) is able to give cave details. Information about speleological centres at Domme and Vézac is given at the end of the Black Périgord chapter.

Cycling

Boot racks with clusters of cycles are a common sight on cars approaching the Dordogne. Rail companies and airlines also readily transport cycles. Main railway stations in the Dordogne have cycles available for hire and there are at least 20 other cycle-hire centres in the region.

Maps with suggested itineraries for cyclists and details of suitable gîtes d'étape are available from railway stations and from the Information Centre in Périgueux. **The Cyclists' Touring Club**, Cotterell House, 69 Meadow House, Goldalming,

Surrey GU7 3HS (☎ 01483 687 217) can provide details of cycling opportunities in the area.

The French take their cycling very seriously: I once waited half-an-hour for service at a pavement café in St-Cyprien whilst the proprietor watched TV coverage of the Tour de France at the bar with his locals.

Fishing

There are plenty of opportunities for fishing in the lakes and streams of the Dordogne region. A licence (carte de pêche) is required and there are restrictions on the size of catch. Some species are protected at particular times of year. Details and licences are available from the Tourist Information Centre in Périgueux (☎ 05 5335 1561) and also from some cafés.

Golf

Golf courses where visitors are welcome are to be found at: Marsac sur L'Isle, near Périgueux; Monestier, near Bergerac; St Félix, near Le Bugue, Mauleydier, near Lalinde; and Vitrac, near Sarlat.

Hôtel du Golf de Castelnaud at Castelnaud de Gratecambe (☎ 05 3016 019), in the Lot region, just south of the Dordogne, offers golfing holidays.

Horse riding

Much of the terrain in Périgord is ideal for horse riding and there are plenty of centres that offer group outings, longer expeditions, instruction and Poney Clubs.

Large centres include: Angie's Ranch, at Tourtoirac; Centre Équestre de Favard, at Tamniès; Le Haras de la Forêt, and L'Étrier de Vitrac, just south of Sarlat.

Other equestrian centres are located at: Bourdeilles; Castelnaud; Hautefort; Jumilhac-le-Grand; Monbazillac; St-Laurent-des-Hommes.

Details are given in the Additional Information guides at the end of each chapter.

Hot-air ballooning

I have myself only ascended in a tethered balloon, but I am sure an untethered flight in a hot-air balloon would be a wonderful way to see the magical countryside of the Dordogne.

Trips can be made from **Montgolfière du Périgord** at La Roque-Gageac (☎ 05 5328 1858).

Parachuting

For those who prefer aerial descending to ascending, parachuting trips can be arranged through the aero club at Bergerac (☎ 05 5357 9809). The Loisirs Accueil at Bergerac will even arrange whole vacations with parachuting as the main activity.

Swimming

Although the Dordogne is an inland region, there are plenty of opportunities for swimming. Many towns and villages, campsites, holiday complexes and hotels have excellent indoor and outdoor pools. Swimming is also permitted in some of the lakes and rivers. Signs give clear warning of any dangerous currents.

Tennis

I often wonder why the French have not produced more champions at tennis, because tennis courts are ubiquitous. Most towns, many villages, including very small ones, virtually all holiday complexes, and many campsites and hotels have courts.

From personal experience, I would advise visitors to book courts for early morning or late afternoon sessions, as I have found playing tennis in the heat of the afternoon sun to be so perspiring that I have worried that it could be expiring!

Walking

Périgord, with terrain that is neither too mountainous nor too flat, is ideal walking territory and is very well served indeed by the excellent Grande Randonnée walking routes. The Grandes Randonnées (GR) are long-distance footpaths which pass through some of the best landscapes and close to many of the well-known attractions. They are served along the way by gîtes d'étapes and other possibilities for overnight accommodation. These are very clearly marked and numbered on the Dordogne Carte Touristique de l'Espace et du Patrimonie which can be obtained from the French Tourist Offices listed above.

The GR6, GR36 and GR64, which all pass through the region, are clearly marked with red and white signposts. The Rando Guide, published by the Comité National des Sentiers de Grandes Ran-données can be obtained from the French Tourist Office in Piccadilly, London (☎ 0207 4919995) and the Dordogne tourist map published by World Leisure have all the GR routes clearly marked.

Shorter walks can be taken on the Petites Randonnées, signposted, according to increasing length, in blue, yellow or green. The Tourist Office in Sarlat (☎ 05 5331 4545) markets a guide with 25 itineraries of varying length.

Water sports

The Grand Étang de la Jemaye, in the heart of the Forêt de la Double, has been set up as a water sports centre. There is equipment for hire and there are picnic areas and basic refreshment facilities on the lakeside. Windsurfing is also available at Tamniès, beteen Les Eyzies and Montignac, and water skiers are catered for at Trémolat.

Some other centres are listed in the free Périgord Découvert brochure and, for those who are prepared to make a special trip, there is a major water sports centre at the Lac de Vassivière, east of Limoges, on the northern edge of Périgord.

Postage

Stamps (timbres) can be purchased from post offices, which normally open from 8am to 7pm on weekdays and 8am to 12 noon on Saturdays. Post offices in smaller centres may close for lunch.

Public Holidays

The following public holidays apply in France:

New Year's Day	
Easter Monday	
May Day	
Ascension Day	
VE Day	(8th May)
Whit Monday	
Bastille Day	(4th July)
Assumption Day	(15th August)
	(Note some attractions close on this day)
All Saints' Day	(1st November)
	(This day marks the end of the season for many attractions)
Armistice Day	(11th November)
Christmas Day	

Telephones

Most public telephones in France do not take coins. They have to be fed with telephone cards (télécartes), which can be obtained from any tabac.

To phone home, leave off the first zero of your home number and prefix the number with the appropriate international code:

Great Britain	00 44
Canada	00 1
USA	00 1

Time

France is one hour ahead of Greenwich Mean Time.

Tipping

Expectations on tipping in restaurants and hotels are similar to those at home, but guides in castles and museums generally expect a small tip.

Tourist Information Centres

Tourist Information Centres and syndicats d'initiative are listed in the Additional Information guides at the end of each chapter. French Tourist Offices abroad are as follows:

Great Britain	**Canada**	**USA**
178 Piccadilly	1981 Avenue McGill College	610 Fifth Avenue Suite 222
London,	Tour Esso Suite 490	New York
W1V 0AL	Montreal, Quebec	NY 10020-2452.
☎ 0207 491 7622	H3 A2 W9.	☎ 212 7571683
	☎ 514 2884 264	

Travelling to the Dordogne

By car

Crossing the Channel

As autoroutes to the south of France now run straight from the port of Calais and also directly from the Channel Tunnel exit, the short crossing is probably the best option for tourists travelling independently to the Dordogne.

Eurotunnel (☎ 0990 353535) operates services every 15 minutes from Folkestone to Calais. The journey through the Channel Tunnel takes about 35 minutes.

P&O Stena (☎ 0990 980980), and **Sea France** (☎ 0990 711711) operate ferry crossings which take about 90 minutes. **Hoverspeed** (☎ 0990 240241) runs a hovercraft service which takes about 35 minutes and a sea cat which crosses in about 50 minutes.

Brittany Ferries (☎ 0990 360360) and Normandy services run by **P&O European Ferries** (☎ 0870 2424999) offer longer, but viable alternatives, especially for those people who regard the sea crossing as part of their holiday. Brittany Ferries run from Poole to Cherbourg, Portsmouth to Caen and St Malo, and Plymouth to Roscoff. P&O European Ferries run from Portsmouth to Cherbourg and Le Havre.

The route to the Dordogne

Large numbers of British tourists travel to the Dordogne by car, many towing a caravan or pulling a trailer laden with a tent. The journey takes about two days.

For motorists entering France by the Channel Tunnel or the Dover-Calais ferry, the most obvious route to the Dordogne is via the A16 autoroute to Paris, the A20 motorway, known as L'Occitane, to Limoges, and then by the N21 (route nationale) to Périgueux. Entry into the Dordogne region is marked for motorists by a sudden profusion of placenames ending in -ac (a Gallo-Roman suffix meaning 'belonging to' or 'the estate of') and a plethora of roadside advertisements for foie gras.

An alternative route takes the motorist to Rouen via the A28, then south along the N154 to Tours, followed by the N143 to Châteauroux where L'Occitane can be picked up. This route has the disadvantage of long non-motorway stretches where slow-moving agricultural vehicles are always liable to cause considerable tailbacks, but offers drivers the opportunity to avoid the Périphérique, the very fast and busy Paris ring road which is somewhat intimidating to some motorists (especially those towing large caravans). The N145 also provides motorists with one of the most memorable views in France: a distant prospect of Chartres Cathedral. Although the church is situated in the middle of the town of Chartres, it appears to stand in isolation in the vast wheatfields.

Motorists entering France at le Havre will probably drive to Évreux to pick up the N154; those disembarking at Caen are probably best advised to take the N158 and N138 to Le Mans and Tours; motorists entering at St Malo may wish to pick up the N138 at Le Mans or travel cross-country to Poitiers.

Motorway driving

Motorway driving in France has its drawbacks, chief of which is the cost of tolls (péage). However, an experiment designed to ease congestion was introduced in 1999; this allows a caravan and car combination travelling on Tuesday, Wednesday or Thursday to use the motorway at the same toll rate as a car, and L'Occitane is currently free of tolls (only until brand loyalty is established?). Slip roads are often rather alarmingly short; hard shoulders are ludicrously narrow and offer little protection for motorists who have breakdowns; most autoroutes are two-lane only and there is often little warning of roadworks, lane switches and motorway splits. When leaving the motorway at service stations, it is important to remember that fuel stations precede refreshment areas (the reverse of the arrangement at British service stations).

However, French autoroutes also have distinct advantages over their British counterparts. Traffic is relatively light, drivers are well protected, by barriers or by shrubbery or vegetation in the central reservation, against the lights of oncoming vehicles, and there are lots of pleasant rest stops (aires) with toilets, picnic areas and telephones.

Driving regulations

All vehicles must carry a red warning triangle and spare headlight bulb. Headlight deflectors for right-hand drive cars can be obtained at outlets near channel terminals.

It is compulsory for front seat passengers to wear seatbelts and children below the age of 10 are not allowed to travel in the front seats.

Speed limits are as follows:

Autoroutes (motorways): 130kph (81 mph) in dry conditions; 110kph (68mph) when wet.

Routes Nationales (N roads): 110kph in dry conditions; 90kph (56mph) when wet.

Other roads: 90kph (56mph) in dry conditions; 80kph (50mph) when wet.

In built-up areas: 50kph (31mph) in dry conditions; 50kph (31mph) when wet.

There are strict on-the-spot impositions for speeding and drink-driving.

Tolls (péage) are charged on most motorways, but not on motorways on the approach to major towns and cities. There are mid-week reductions for car and caravan outfits.

The infamous rule of priorité à droite (give way to traffic from the right) has disappeared from main roads, but still applies on unmarked junctions, including those in built-up areas. Also, the rule no longer applies at roundabouts (except at L'Étoile in Paris!); motorists must now give way to traffic already on the roundabout.

Nationals of EU countries require a valid Driving Licence, but American and Canadian drivers require an International Driving Licence.

Above: Relaxing on a caravan holiday

Below: A selection of the Dordogne's many show caves

Fuel

Fuel is sold as super, sans plomb (unleaded), gazole (diesel), and prices are comparable with those in the UK, but diesel is currently one third cheaper.

By coach

A number of companies offer coach tours which include the Dordogne in their itineraries and National Express coaches operate a Euroline service (☎ 0207 7308235) to Périgueux and Bordeaux. In many ways, coach travel is an attractive option: modern coaches have a controlled environment and excellent facilities; the driver takes the strain; there is none of the hassle associated with changing trains and passengers have a comfortable seat with a wonderful elevated view of the countryside. However, long-haul coach travel can be quite tiring. The sense of confinement doesn't help: coach passengers have less freedom of movement than rail passengers and, unlike motorists, they do not have the option of stopping as the mood takes them.

By train

It is now possible to travel from Waterloo to Bordeaux in about 9 hours, using **Eurostar** (☎ 0990 186186) with a link to the very fast TGV service at Lille. Tickets can be obtained from some 200 rail stations throughout the UK.

Motorail (☎ 08705 848848) operates an overnight service from Calais to Brive, with sleeping compartments or shared couchettes. Let the train take the strain!

By air

British Airways (☎ 0345 222111) flies three times per day from Gatwick to Bordeaux and Toulouse; flight time is about 2hrs 30mins.

Air France (☎ 0208 742 6600) flies from Heathrow to Toulouse, and also has four flights per day from Edinburgh, Glasgow, Newcastle, Manchester and Birmingham to Bordeaux via Paris.

Passengers arriving at Bordeaux are faced with a 2hrs 30mins drive into the Dordogne itself, but there are car rental centres at Bordeaux, with a range of models from 4-seaters to 7-seater people carriers.

Details are available from:
Hertz (☎ 0990 906090)
Skycars (☎ 01923 835317)
Avis (☎ 0990 900500).

Travelling in the Dordogne

There is a reasonable train network in the Dordogne area and there are pretty good local bus services. Tourists intending to use these services would be well advised to consult tourist offices for full details, in order to plan their itineraries in advance.

Wonderful ways in which to see the Dordogne include walking along the

Grandes Randonnées, cycling along the many cycle tracks and the quieter roads, horse riding on the bridle paths, and canoeing along the region's rivers. (See above under 'Outdoor Activities', and also in the Additional Information at the end of each chapter.)

Tourists who are keen to make a general tour of Périgord are advised to use a car. The Dordogne region is away from the main motorway network and there only a few wide N roads, but there is a very good network of D roads. These are generally well surfaced but often narrow and flanked by ditches, so it is important to take care when you are pulling over to allow another vehicle to pass! Two other hazards should be mentioned: French drivers seem to regard overtaking as a challenge, not least on blind bends, so motorists, and their passenger-navigators, should have their wits about them; D roads often pass through thickly wooded areas with occasional clearings, so sudden changes from deep shadow to brilliant light often present a problem.

D roads also seem to change their number designations with unnecessary frequency, so a good map is essential. Michelin maps are excellent and the AA Road Atlas of France covers the road network in minute detail, but good eyesight is essential for reading it!

Visas

No entry visa is required by American or Canadian visitors staying in France for less than 3 months.

Index

Index

Published in the UK by
Landmark Publishing Ltd
Ashbourne Hall, Cokayne Avenue, Ashbourne, Derbyshire DE6 1EJ England
☎ 01335 347349 E-mail landmark@clara.net Web-site www.landmarkpublishing.co.uk

Published in the USA by
Hunter Publishing Inc
222 Clematis Street, West Palm Beach FL 33401 USA
☎ 001 561 835 2022 E-mail: michael@hunterpublishing.com

2nd Edition

ISBN 13: 978-1-84306-166-3
ISBN 10: 1-84306-166-X

© **Mike Smith 2007**
The right of Mike Smith as author of this work has been asserted by him in
accordance with the Copyright, Design and Patents Act, 1993.

All rights reserved. No part of this publication may be reproduced, stored in a retrieval
system or transmitted in any form or by any means, electronic, mechanical,
photocopying, recording or otherwise without the prior
permission of Landmark Publishing Ltd.

British Library Cataloguing in Publication Data: a catalogue record for this
book is available from the British Library.

Print: Cromwell Press, Trowbridge
Design & Cartography: James Allsopp
Editor: Pat Fielding

Front cover: Biron Castle
Back cover, top: Shooting the rapids, Brantôme
Back cover, bottom: Canoes on the Dordogne, La Roque Gageac

Picture Credits
The photographs have been supplied by the author.

DISCLAIMER

While every care has been taken to ensure that the information in this book
is as accurate as possible at the time of publication, the publishers
and authors accept no responsibility for any loss, injury or inconvenience
sustained by anyone using this book.